For She Who Leads

Practical Wisdom from a Woman Who Serves

Written by Holly J. McIlwain, MS

For She Who Leads
Practical Wisdom from a Woman Who Serves

Editor: Shelley Kleysteuber
Graphic Designer: Andrea Grieco, AndreaGriecoDesign.com
Photographer: Jordan Sweeney, JordanLouisePhoto.com

ISBN 978-1-945605-03-1

I can think of few female friends and colleagues with whom these stories will not resonate. *For She Who Leads* explores the challenges—and exposes the myths—that so many of us face on our hero's journey to conquer all. Regardless of whether you define yourself as a breadwinner, a mother, a partner, or a daughter/sister/friend, Holly's recounting of her struggles while attempting to obtain perfection will resonate with you, and her story of overcoming (and accepting imperfection) will inspire!

— Lisa Hernandez, Esq.
Chief Human Resources Officer, Robert Morris University
Wife, mother, daughter, sister, former litigator and recovering perfectionist

Her Europe backpacking trip, his car, the family's matching Christmas pajamas, the Instagram life of luxury, the perfect life of "someone else"...we all fall victim to the ruse of comparison. Our 26th President Theodore (Teddy) Roosevelt once said (errr the bible first actually) that comparison is the thief of joy. During Teddy's tenure he realized that the pressure of who had come before him and what was expected of him within such a royal position. But Roosevelt knew something then that some of us often struggle with today...comparison takes away the joy from who you are, what you have, and what you do. So how do we get from this state of comparison to this state of contentment? There are ways to keep comparison shoved in the bottom of the drawer, pushed to the back of the closet, stuffed under the bed, or if you are intentional with your practices...dropped off completely at the local Goodwill. *For She Who Leads* offers a thoughtful and personal story of how to manage comparison through efficient and thoughtful techniques. From re-establishing your values, to drawing boundaries, and mastering the art of tug of war when it comes to letting go or holding on. After reading this "joyful but raw" book you'll be ready to arm wrestle with all of that shame, fear, and comparison that's been lurking under your bed. Get ready to fight the monster impostors that live in us all.

— Tera McIntosh, Ph.D.
Atlantic University, Mindful Leadership Program
Professor, avid coffee drinker and recovering "fixer and not enough-er"

Those who want to lead must also have a strong desire to serve, to allow themselves to find the best in others in order to really unleash the best in themselves. Holly McIlwain understands, embodies, and promotes these concepts and inspires those around her with her willingness to be completely open and share her experiences with her readers. *For She Who Leads* is a read that will illuminate the challenges of driving yourself and others to greatness, and you will read it from start to finish multiple times!

— Shannon J. Gregg

President, Cloud Adoption Solutions and Co-Author of *It's About Time*
Salesforce lover, mom jazz dancer and almost-Ph.D.

Holly presents a powerful message to all women to silence the brutal self-criticism that is brought on by ongoing internal head chatter and to realize that you are enough as you are. *For She Who Leads* presents with vivid imagery through eloquent prose that every woman owns a combination of unique talent, strength and wisdom carefully crafted to be celebrated and shared.

— Ann Gatty, Ph.D.

President, Strategic People Solutions and Author of *Leadership Unleashed*
Wife, mother, daughter, sister and failed Superwoman with scars proudly displayed

Contents

Preface

This is the book…
That needs to be written.
That begs to be read.
That tells the story of hard work. Lots of hard work.
And of marriage, and children, and partnerships, and mentorships,
and dreaming, and parenting, and success, and failure, and tears.

It is the book that tells the truth about women who are leading—in business, in families, in communities all over the country. Who have largely been silent, so I will tell their stories. I've asked some of these women to tell it in their own words, because words matter. Names matter. It all matters. Which is why I didn't want to write this book. I really didn't want to write this book. Carving out the time in my already too busy life to write this seemed next to impossible. Every time I spoke to a room full of women about journeys and hope and sadness and success and the struggle that wraps every part of that up for me, I walked away with a little more of the ache to tell the story. The whole story. Not just my story, but Shannon's story, Mary's story, Neysha's story, Tina's story, Kelly's story. The real story is heard in the voices of the women I get to look at and live in the same community with…and to shine lights on the incredible women in history who made this possible to even script.

I didn't want to write this book. But every conversation that pushed me for honesty and truth and to show my scars opened a new page and pulled the words from me. Thank you to these women, and men, who listened and laughed with and at me as the stories were being told and happening around us! Thank you to my mentors and professional "boss babes", whose business acumen, honesty, and integrity stretch me and make me brave. Thank you to my tribe of powerful women who rally around me, show up and throw down—you make me fun again. Thank you to my childhood friends who continue to inspire me and provide comfort in "being known". Thank you to my mother and aunts and cousins and sister who played such huge roles in helping me understand the layers and layers of women whom I share DNA with! Thank you to my father for showing me love and support in the most significant moments—even in silence. Thank you to my incredible husband for speaking truth to me and for choosing me, and for being strong, but mostly for making me a mother. Thank you to my smart, funny, thoughtful sons who light up my everyday and make me want to be better and better for you. James and John, never be afraid to follow a strong woman.

Now the hard work begins. This is the book you need to read because it is about overcoming the standard idea of "having it all" and defining "having it all" for yourself. There are so many versions of "having it all" out there; impostor syndrome runs deep. Call it social media inundation, call it the human condition. Call it whatever you like. The truth is, some studies say that up to 70% of all people will experience this phenomenon at work.

This phenomenon shows up in some strangely unremarkable ways, and sadly, it is largely unreported, undiscovered, and unacknowledged by women until they hear someone else talking about it. Someone they admire, trust, respect, or know to be authentically talented. Let me be clear here: I'm not putting myself on a pedestal, but I am shouting, LOUD AND CLEAR, that I can relate to these and have battled with more than one of them. So this is your group session. I am speaking out. If you battle this venomous, nasty little voice, then let's fight her together.

The four fears, as I have discovered, relate to impostor syndrome and what the implications are:

1. Fear of being discovered as less intelligent or talented than she really is, resulting in an endless (and thankless) cycle of hard work and overcompensation. The harder she works, the more success she experiences, and the more she fears being discovered as a talentless hack. So she works harder, harbors resentment, and teeters on burnout.

2. Fear of being discovered as more intelligent or talented than everyone else, resulting in intellectual inauthenticity as she is not speaking up and often allowing others to take credit for her contributions. She persists in this space, placing others in the spotlight and working harder and harder to advance quietly, so that she is undiscovered. She doesn't take the risk, she steps aside, out of the line.

3. Fear of being ordinary and using perceptiveness (and manipulation) to place herself outside the pack by winning the attention and approval of the key decision maker or power player in a dynamic, resulting in a version of phoniness that is imperceptible to her and caustic to others. Unfortunately, if she is good at obtaining this external validation, she doubts it and moves on to a new target. She's never satisfied with her own success.

4. Fear of succeeding and being set apart by her own abilities. Which is the saddest one, I think. As Pauline Rose Clance succinctly offers, "To maintain a sense of herself as being an intellectual phony may allow a high achieving woman to live out her achievement orientation to a large degree and at the same time allay some of her fears about the negative consequences of being a successful woman in our society."[1]

I recently read an article[2] that helped me understand how widespread impostor syndrome really is. Virtually every person who experiences success in some way also experiences impostor syndrome. But because we are all so different, the way that a person is affected by it looks different. A team of researchers went after this in a university setting (because you know, college students are willing subjects and highly accessible—but why researchers have to mess with them in their frequently emotionally unstable state I do not know...). These scientists took hundreds of undergrads and worked to make sure that the students were having a seriously miserable failure of a day. They framed it as a GRE exam, and for half of the students, gave them fake feedback that created a deeper sense of failure. The pressure grew among the group and the games continued. The students responded differently based on gender; male students tended to crumble under the weight of failure and chose not to invest their time in the test, succumbing to the feedback as a self-actualizing prophecy. The female students, on the other hand, increased their efforts and showed superior performance. They had the same feelings of disappointment and dread, but they were able to overcome them. This research study blew my mind. As if dealing with menstruation and childbearing weren't impressive enough, coupled with the amazing way that even our FACES learn ways to grow hair after a certain age, women are incredible. We can receive poor feedback, be actively made miserable with a shit day, and still kick ass on a task? Yes. Yes, we can. And for she who leads, this must be remembered. Impostor syndrome is a product of all the external factors and cannot limit you if you do not allow it to. But you have to spend time getting to know who you are and what you are capable of before stepping on that lie.

So, who is this woman in the mirror?

Okay, truth talk. I've lived with the reality of impostor syndrome for years and years—especially early in my career, but if I'm being honest, it still creeps in.

I never knew it was an actual "thing" until recently. The thought that I was "lucky" or "blessed" to be in the job that I was in, the change happening that I was invited to something and an opportunity opened up...blah, blah, blah.

The truth was, when I looked at that woman in the mirror, I didn't think she deserved the level of success that was within her reach. And sometimes I didn't let her reach for it. I held her back. I felt like the impostor.

So what is impostor syndrome and how does it impact the ability of women like you and me to achieve what we were created for?

Impostor syndrome shows up among seemingly confident, high-functioning, intelligent women (and sometimes men), manifesting as pervasive feelings of insecurity, self-doubt, and the fear of being revealed as a fraud and unmasked as incompetent. Actual competence and ability are not objective factors, acknowledged and measured by success or notable accomplishments. This fear of being found out as worthless or a hack lies quietly in wait as success builds. A promotion is earned, a book is published, a benchmark is met...and then it emerges and upends the stability that success of this level should bring.

Two researchers who have spent a great deal of time investigating impostor syndrome are Pauline Rose Clance and Suzanne Imes. Pauline herself experienced symptoms of impostor syndrome in graduate school and withheld her feelings of anxiety, fear, and self-doubt from even her friends. It sparked something that has garnered a wider body of research, and she and Suzanne coined the phrase "impostor phenomenon", describing it in their own words as affecting women with the following thought pattern:

> "Even though they are often very successful by external standards, they feel their success has been due to some mysterious fluke or luck or great effort; they are afraid their achievements are due to 'breaks' and not the result of their own ability and competence. They are also pretty certain that, unless they go to gargantuan efforts to do so, success can not be repeated. They are afraid that next time, I will blow it."[3]

In their earliest work in this area, Pauline Rose Clance and Suzanne Imes explain the phenomenon from a clinical perspective. "The Impostor Phenomenon in High Achieving Women: Dynamics and Therapeutic Intervention" effectively launches a deeper dive into the topic for dozens of independent studies, and perhaps more importantly, giving validation to these feelings that so many seemingly successful women were already dealing with. Imagine getting up and going into work every day, managing a team and meeting performance expectations. You have a good job, by all accounts. A nice home. Decent nail beds. A significant project comes your way—it will be one of those stretch projects, one that requires a little more from you, but will certainly bring with it additional opportunities and recognition, and launch you and your work team into the spotlight for a job well done. You worked hard. Your put in extra hours, made extra calls, and provided your team Chick-Fil-A lunches on more than one occasion, in order to bolster their confidence in the good job they are doing. In fact, you make recognition part of your management style, so those team members who are pulling extra weight are even getting appropriate kudos from you. When the project is finally completed, and you are recognized by the entire company for successful completion, you begin to sweat. A nagging question lingers in the back of your mind: *When will they discover that I am incompetent?* And when asked how you accomplished this feat in the pressed time window you were given, you respond, "I was lucky to have such a great team." While this seems humble and very "we" not "I" oriented, it is an outward projection of some of those Impostor Phenomenon indicators that Pauline and Suzanne discovered and named. Even more disturbing is what might happen to a woman over time if this behavior and thought pattern goes on unchecked. In this benchmark paper explaining the dynamics and therapeutic interventions, they make two distinct assertions:

1. Women who experience the impostor phenomenon maintain a strong belief that they are not intelligent; in fact they are convinced that they have fooled anyone who thinks otherwise.

2. Women who exhibit the impostor phenomenon do not fall into any one diagnostic category. The clinical symptoms most frequently reported are generalized anxiety, lack of self-confidence, depression, and frustration related to inability to meet self-imposed standards of achievement.[1]

This was interesting to me as I began researching in earnest for this book. My fried had shared with me studies showing that women simply didn't position themselves for promotions because they would look at the list of seven or eight needed competencies and see that they were missing one or two, while men at this same professional level were more likely to go after them despite having far fewer key competencies! That was amazing to me, but then I sat back and reflected on some of my own experiences and observations and understood it. Pauline Rose Clance and Suzanne Imes point out this inherent difference which shows up between women and men: men often view their own successes as resultative of qualities they have within themselves, whereas women are more likely to attribute their success elsewhere; they will "either project the cause of success outward to an external cause (luck) or to a temporary internal quality (effort) that they do not equate with inherent ability."[1].

It seems like this impostor phenomenon, gone unchecked for too long, becomes a syndrome impacting women so significantly that a growing professional circuit of coaches, therapists, and mentors are identifying it and helping women work through it. Core to avoiding, overcoming, or recovering from the impostor syndrome that creeps in on, say about 70% of us, is truly understanding yourself, what you're worth, and what you want most. The chapters you will read will push you to define this. You may not want to do so in the book itself, especially if you're the "pass a book along" kind of friend that we all love. In that case, start up a document you can access anywhere, and start writing using the prompts. Shoot, perhaps this will result in your own book. Please, please, please send me my very own copy. I love this shit. What I love even more than that is knowing that you're going to do something with this very lovely piece of work.

What to expect as you move through the book:

1. Establishing *your* values and creating boundaries to protect what you hold most dear.

2. Knowing when to push harder, and when to rest for a bit.

3. Recognizing when to work on the long run (marathon) versus sprinting through the quick takes.

4. Training and conditioning to be a working mother/caregiver/hobbyist/partner/pet owner.

5. Rest and rejuvenation is necessary every day—the idea of restoration of the Sabbath is good food for thought for she who leads. Even God rested on the seventh day. Why don't we?!

6. Questioning the who in "Whose vision are we seeing?" Ours? Our boss's? Our spouse's? Some social construct? Why is it necessary to understand the vision? And why should you create space for one of your own?

Through this body of your own thoughts and journaling and discussing with friends and peers, and in putting in the work of applying the stuff that makes the most sense to you and for you (no impostors please). People matter, you matter, this matters.

People are not objects, and should not be used. Especially as a means to some end.

Coping doesn't work. We might feel like coping is "rising above" and powering through, but it doesn't solve the actual problems, and that won't work for long. We have to see people as people, not as problems to overcome.

Applying the stuff isn't a system or checklist, but a way to think deeply about who you are, and whose you are. You may be employed, but you are not the property of your company. You may be a wife and mother, but you are still you. Even when your body doesn't look like the one you know. Even when your soul doesn't feel like the person you remember. There is a woman leading. Who are you and how do *you* serve?

For She Who Leads is a look inside the souls of women in motion—me, and you. Let's stop moving long enough to take this in, and make the next steps intentional. For she who leads is not motivated by fear or frenzy, so together we step forward with hope and harmony. Ready for the first steps?

Introduction

"The one person who will never leave us, whom we will never lose, is ourself. Learning to love our female selves is where our search for love must begin."
— bell hooks, Communion: The Female Search for Love[4]

On August 18, 1920, the 19th Amendment was added to the U.S. Constitution, declaring that women would have the right to vote from that day forward. For centuries prior, women had been growing and grooming generations upon generations of educators, presidents, kings, world leaders, thinkers, inventors, innovators, explorers, scientists, mathematicians, physicians, physicists, laborers, judges, writers, and literally every other person making a contribution to society of any kind. The world could not and would not go on without the contributions of women—physically developing the next generation and giving birth to our future, and socially providing for the care and upbringing of the young and old. This raises the question of why are we, 100 years beyond the 19th Amendment, still grappling with the ability to have our voices heard and valued in our homes, workplaces, and in society?

For she who leads, the first battle is in answering the question "Am I enough?" Beyond the initial question, it becomes "What is enough?" None of this is easy. None of this is static. Even for the women who, more than a hundred years ago, worked so hard to declare the equality and dignity of women, factions broke them apart and so many starts and stops slowed progress. For more recent generations, the sexual revolution crashed into the #MeToo movement, bra burning destroyed pure femininity, and women's liberation in the workplace caused mothers to fear the dreaded call from daycare. All of this, fracture among fracture, getting us off course. When we dare to put everything on the table, and recognize that all brands of femaleness matter, and have dignity, and are worthwhile contributions to society and the conversation, something happens. The women we most admire, the women on these pages, the women who have remarkable and unremarkable stories, all matter. Agreement on all fronts is not a necessity for recognition. For she who leads, everything matters.

Enter Lucy Burns, Vassar College and Yale University-educated suffragette who learned civil disobedience by fighting alongside the women uprising in Great Britain years earlier. Lucy was mentored by other women, wives and mothers with daughters and sisters, like Emmeline Pankhurst, fighting in the UK. This earned Lucy some notoriety, being named in the newspapers for "disorderly conduct" related to her activism. Stateside, Lucy Burns had other close companions she labored with—organizing protests, drafting letters, and inciting women of all ages to step into the ring and fight for the right to use their voices for more than singing lullabies and asking if he wanted pie with his coffee. Lucy fought alongside Dorothy Day, but is far less widely known in the suffragette movement. Did Lucy's father, the Catholic father of eight children who believed that his daughters should receive the same opportunity for college education as his sons, ever expect that his daughter would change the world? Maybe. He likely expected it to be through marrying well and bearing a boatload of children. He likely never expected that his Lucy would spend more time in prison than any other suffrage activist. Imprisonment for women at this time was abysmal—rat-infested, torturesome, unimaginable conditions. Lucy's imprisonment included being force-fed a nutritional substance by mouth while her nose was held shut during a 19-day hunger strike. Lucy's "Night of Terror", November 15, 1917, sparked something in many women and men, and after her release she spoke of it widely and brought on more and more activists willing to join the fight to allow women the right to vote.[5]

Such brutality and aggression directed towards the women who fought, and continued to fight after suffering abuse, thinking all the time of you and of me, women who 100 years later are still fighting. Our battle looks a little different now, as we are battling with ourselves and each other about what it means to have it all, to achieve balance and harmony. We battle with our employers and competitors, to be taken seriously in business, to experience equal pay for equal experience, and to *not* be asked to take the notes at every meeting. We battle with the media for the right to be healthy and whole and beautiful at any size, shape, and color, to be more than a body. This list goes on and on.

When we stop and account for what have we done to fight for the next generation of women, who will be the women, like Lucy Burns and her compatriots, whose names will be written on pages like this? With women making up just over half of the population of the United States, the continuation of underrepresentation in leadership roles is alarming. A look through the top 100 CEOs of companies in the United States[6] is an exercise in frustration, as women on the list are few and far between. So what do we make of that? Lucy's story isn't unlike the stories you will read in this book. For she who leads, courage and strength are in her DNA.

While we've held on to some of the rights Lucy and her sister suffragettes fought for, there are other issues still on the table. Gender parity shines a light on the closing wage gap between men and women in the same roles, yet women still a significant portion of unpaid labor on the home front. #MeToo has broken wide open the issues of sexual harassment and abuse, given women who suffered as victims the voice needed to change the tide, while at the same time giving justification for more male business leaders to shut women out of the tough conversations, claiming fear of future (unfounded) accusations. We still have a lot of work to do.

The unintended side effects of the #MeToo movement have been a topic of discussion in just about every industry and region, so much so that *USA Today* compiled the research over the past year to reveal some harrowing statistics. This data points to some observable behaviors in the workplace—a space where diversity conversations have been squelched by risk management instead. "The confusion stems from cultural differences in a country as vast and diverse as the United States. What may be regarded as an inoffensive hug or compliment in one setting could be interpreted as a come-on in another," reports *USA Today* contributor Jorge L. Ortiz.[7]

Between LeanIn.org and Pew Research, polls conducted in 2018 revealed that 66 percent of older adults (65+) believe that men have more difficulties in navigating workplace interactions, resulting in fewer women hired for roles that closely engage with the men in senior leadership. This means fewer executive roles for women, fewer opportunities for advancement, and more excuses to justify sexism. These studies aren't limited to the behaviors and attitudes of older men in the workplace though. More than half of Americans hold the belief that the increased focus on #MeToo and sexual harassment and assault have made it more difficult for men to know how to interact with women at work. Rather than treating women as equals with respect, more and more men hold back feedback, shy away from mentoring, and keep their distance.

The value in taking wide and deep looks at the societal impact and implications of the women pioneering changes in the Suffragette movement, on the front lines of identifying impostor phenomenon and treating impostor syndrome, and protecting women from future abuse with #MeToo is that we have always been able to change things for the next generations by enduring the hard things of the present. Women have built into their bodies and brains and wiring the incredible power to sustain difficulties and push through pain—persevering with the grit and grace that I am grateful to have had opportunities to grow in. On a basic biological level, the very act of growing a child in the womb and giving birth is so natural to us, providing reminders of the power to create change and push forth progress for the future of humanity. A step further, understanding and observing that even our monthly menstrual cycle is a reminder to us of the power we hold. Adopting this perspective certainly overturns this notion that women are "the weaker sex". We are not. We do hard things. We make new life. We bleed for five days and keep going. Look at us—we are incredible. Now is the time for women to step up and step into the incredible power we hold, using grit to display grace.

THINK IT OUT

Discussion/Reflection Questions

Who are the brave, strong women you see leading? What are their stories? If you don't know, now is the time to ask…and to tell your own story.

Your story begins with acknowledging your personal history. Identify five key moments that have led you to this moment in your life—personally and professionally/vocationally.

What is something you are proud of from your own personal history—something you did or made happen?

What is the one thing you need to be brave about in your life right now?

SOMETHING TO PONDER

"Above all, be the heroine of your life, not the victim."

— Nora Ephron[8]

Not all women are tasked with the suffering that Lucy Burns and her counterparts, the Suffragettes, experienced. Here we are, 100 years later, with an opportunity to be brave in totally relevant, yet not entirely new ways. Lucy's personal history, as much as your own, gives us the grit and grace to step forward.

CHAPTER 1

Know Thyself

The last time you leave a place lingers with you a bit. It was a Tuesday morning, not terribly cold but brisk enough to require a coat. My keys always stayed in the pocket of my coat when I was at work. My first appointment of the day canceled, so I had a little time for digital housekeeping before meeting with my boss and his partner. The air was thicker than usual in the office, and I felt that unfamiliar feeling that no one wants to meet: dread.

Things had been off; I felt it. My greatest strength—connectedness, the belief that everything works together and is part of the same giant whole—is also my greatest weakness. I cannot let any crack exist in the vessel that holds it all together. I've felt it my whole life—I've lived in the space of smoothing over, going beyond, and bending, stretching, doing. I've sat with this need to do more, be more, feel more, give more. I've been undone by the dismemberment of self-assuredness, as the fear of *not being enough* while simultaneously wondering if I might be *too much* became a daily battle. And this unsteady environment was playing into these fears in ways I thought that I had battled and put to death already.

But I hadn't. My big brave movement was leaving a comfortable job in an organization that I loved to embark on a challenging concourse in business. I placed all my eggs in this basket and hadn't seen the results that I was so sure were coming. I was overly optimistic, too trusting, and naive. When the first shoe dropped, I talked myself out of these feelings of doom and angst. As pieces of the ceiling were starting to fall down, I pivoted to provide value. Eventually, the hard work that I was doing to be brave was being misinterpreted as another five-letter "B" word often used to describe a strong willed woman. Not b-o-s-s-y. The other one. But that wasn't me—usually. It wasn't me there. That day. I showed up. When I sat in that conference room, across the table from two men who underestimated me (and most other women and a fair population of men), I allowed the other shoe to drop, and my dread transformed into relief.

Reflecting on that day now, I see that it was the best thing that could have ever happened. Leaving. I had taken on this motto, "Do one scary thing every day", when I began this new role, and used it to track my progress. I did *a lot* of scary things. But I gave those scary things a lot of power and control in my life. As a newish wife, and a totally new mom, I lived in the scary, self-doubting, nearly debilitating space of UGH. And it wasn't pretty.

I left that place with dignity. With my head high. Respectfully, graciously, kindly. Proud of the woman that I had evolved into, and yet realizing that this was the very thing that made the men around me so uncomfortable. I wasn't helpless, torn apart, destroyed. I was choosing the brave thing, in that moment. And that mattered more than any of the words spoken to me, about me, or for me on that last day, or conse-quently in the days that followed. When you know yourself, the volume spoken by the strength to carry on is greater than that of the voices around you.

I have never claimed to be perfect. But I know myself. I will never be as good as I want to be. But I will always be better today than I was yesterday. I will always live in the belief that tomorrow matters. Everything matters.

And this thinking trickles into all kinds of other places. Men, they are perhaps a little more simple, I think. Many men can define themselves by their duty, their accomplishments, their contributions. At the end of the day, the door can be closed on other things because their accomplishments have spoken for themselves. But women, glorious women, complex and feeling monsters, aren't we? We define ourselves by the relationships we cherish—the roles that we play. Ask a man to tell you about himself and he'll tell you what he does—banker, golfer. Ask a woman and she'll tell you who she is in relation to other people. Mother. Wife. Caregiver. Boss lady.

This attachment sometimes challenges common...sense. Because values and desires often carry more weight than common sense and practical wisdom. What we want is usually more attractive than what we need. Case in point: the desire to be loved.

I grew up in a home with hardworking parents, in a small town with good and honest people, and with a knowledge of "good girls don't do that"...whatever "that" might be. The lack of honest conversation hung heavy in the air. There wasn't enough time to sit around talking anyway. There was always more work to do before sundown. As the youngest in the family, I relished the spotlight. I loved making people feel better. I was my mother's constant companion, shadow, and relief from the rest of the pack, for the first five years of my life. I was my dad's joy for the next ten. And by the time high school rolled around, my parents were perhaps too busy with their rediscovered Jesus to pay much attention to me (or my newly married siblings...all of them it seemed had gotten married in a three-year stretch). I tried out different personas, activities, personal styles, relationships, and after school jobs. This fed the lifelong battle of "what is enough" for me—I felt that I needed to earn the love, affection, and attention of those I was encountering and didn't know it. Those habits of high school Holly certainly ran deep. Twenty years later and the same self-doubt can creep in if I'm not paying attention.

Leaving home was big for me. My parents *still* live in the same home that they built and raised a family in. A big farmhouse, out in the country, with handmade wooden tongue and groove pieces crafted by my father's huge calloused hands. Hands that could fix any car, operate any machine, and once delivered a baby cow! My father had the most enormous hands. One of my earliest memories was being four or five, sitting on his lap with both of my little feet nestled inside his enormous hands. In my memory, my dad was always enormous. And he used way too much black pepper on everything he ate. And hated the smell of nail polish remover. And was ridiculously good at English (even though it was his second language) and was forever correcting our grammar. It was annoying. I couldn't wait to leave home at 17.

Leaving home to go to college—breaking some unwritten rule in my family that you only leave home to get married. (I really broke that one—I didn't get married until I was in my 30s. *Really* breaking the family pattern.) I left home and swore I'd never return to the small town that raised me. I started a new life at college, like just about everyone else, right? I got a taste of independence, responsibility, and saw how much hard work paid off. I couldn't wait to do it all. Ultimately, I graduated and went after my dream of changing the world, broke my foot in the upper peninsula of Michigan (long story for another book), and had to move back in with my parents. Like a loser. Well, that's what I thought. I stayed for exactly six months, then got back out to chase my dreams by working 2+ jobs at a time and thinking about how much I could change the world if I kept at it.

I left home again and again and again for a few years. I kept my parents' house key on my keychain, and dropped in often. One of the happiest departures was with my dad—he drove me to my first house closing. I had purchased a house at 24 years old, and we were moving *all* the pieces of my youth into a 1000 square foot piece of heaven that I paid for on my own. My dad was so proud of me for this. He had just retired, so we got to hang out a ton in that house. The day that I closed on that house, the small wooden church that I attended for my whole life back in my hometown burned to the ground. It was one of the happiest and saddest days I'd ever known. But I was young. I'd have a lot more of those days to walk through.

Something a young person should never have to do is drive to their parents' house and tell them that they have cancer. When I sat across the old Formica kitchen table that I had eaten thousands of meals at over the years (and actually hated because it didn't match the kitchen at all), to deliver this news to my parents, I thought that I could actually hear their hearts breaking. It was one of the worst moments I had known. Leaving their home that day, driving back to my little slice of heaven and wondering what the hell was going to happen to me, to them, to everything, was tough.

Having a home to go back to is important—it's where we first learn that we can have a voice. We learn that our words matter. We learn the power of phrases like "I'm sorry", "Thank you," "I love you," "Help me". Going back home to recover and heal after having cancer was important. In some weird way, it was redeeming part of my childhood that got overlooked a little with all the *rediscovering* happening. My mom felt needed again. She held me through every painful treatment. My dad felt strong. He literally lifted me out of bed to use the bathroom. That time was precious. Leaving home after recovering from a couple of cancer surgeries—that was a tough one. My dad suffered a stroke shortly after and it forever changed him, and the way that I was able to think about strength. And influence how I would finally decide who and when to get married. Everything changed, shortly thereafter. But maybe things had been changing all along, and I just didn't know who I was in the midst of it. Those years revealed her to me.

Let me be clear: The woman who wrote this is so imperfect. The woman who wrote this is surviving and striving. I never stopped wanting something more. More for me. More for my sister. My mother. My friends. We don't have time to read these self-help books! But for the women who read this one, and share it, and apply it—these women are the activators. The women who read this are desiring something more, found within themselves and possibly within the pages of this book. But it is not any singular brand of wisdom alone that is promoted. Together our voices reveal *something more*. And this something more allows us all to be better. For she who leads is not alone—she is where she needs to be, with a village of women behind her, an army of warriors beside her, and so many women who have walked before her.

Discussion/Reflection Questions

Home. What are the places that you have left, and return to, that have shaped you? What relationships live there, past or present, that have had an impact on the woman you are today?

Finding your voice, and listening to that voice. Sometimes as women, we feel like we can't speak up or out. Sometimes it's because we fear being *too much, or not* _____ *enough*. Push through those fears in this moment and write down five words that describe the voice that is yours. Who is she, and what is she saying?

1.
2.
3.
4.
5.
What is she saying?

What matters most. When we don't know who we are, and can't pick our own voices, it gets really hard to figure out what steps we need to take. We get wrapped around the axle of all the shoulds, coulds, and woulds. It takes courage to give yourself permission to use that voice.

I have chosen to no longer be apologetic for my femaleness and my femininity. And I want to be respected in all of my femaleness because I deserve to be."

— Chimamanda Ngozi Adichie, *We Should All Be Feminists*[9]

CHAPTER 2

Know Thy Boundaries

I can remember hitting the parking garage after a 9.5 hour day, already checking my email on my smartphone as I took the stairs up to the fourth floor. My space. I was in the office every day at 6:15 a.m., so this coveted space was practically reserved for me. Thinking back, it's some kind of miracle that my stilettos didn't cause a face plant. I was so distracted by achievement that I didn't see the creeping encroachment on my personal space and time that I was allowing my work to have. Before you start thinking that perhaps I had a really powerful job, or was making a ton of money and all of this merited 18+ hours a day of "being on", I didn't and I wasn't. It was my first "formal and professional" role in leadership for my organization—a reputable non-profit that had gone through the wringer. I justified this workaholism by rationalizing two things: 1) I didn't deserve to be there—I didn't have the educational credentials of many of my colleagues and if I messed up, they would figure out that hiring me was a mistake; and 2) Our constituents had already been through so much, I had to overperform to make up for the mistakes of other people.

This chapter is for the woman who knows the lie of having it all and doing it all. The woman who treats boundaries as oxygen and battles to protect them. The woman who thinks about what she needs to give her best to the people and responsibilities she is entrusted with (and to) in an unselfish but self-respecting way.

I suppose it's also for the woman who struggles with all of this and wants to establish something sustainable for herself and the people she reaches. The truth is, our personal histories influence our own ability to define these boundaries and have healthy relationships with others. For better or for worse, so to speak.

Capture the (Red) Flag

Similar to the origins of impostor syndrome, when a woman is repeatedly told that she's too much, too emotional, not business savvy, not smart, etc., it becomes the track that plays in her head and drowns out the naturally occurring warning system that would normally help her capture those red flags and get the hell out of dodge. I am one of those women. Er, I was one of those women. And then I got wise to the game. Of course, it came after an experience of burnout and heartbreak.

Remember the game capture the flag from when we were kids? You divide into teams, form a line, select a guard, identify the target, run like hell in pursuit of the target, dodging traps and trip ups set up by the opponents, and if you get tagged, you're stuck. Oh, and you can only free one person at a time.

This can be translated to professional (and personal) games that people play, so, similar to the game, establishing boundaries allows for all players to know the rules, and the consequences of violating one of these established boundaries. Some people play the game fairly, honoring the rules, and others do not. We know those people in our lives as well, but sometimes struggle to get on the other side of the field and stay away from the people that trip others up and play dirty.

Let's turn to one of the world's leading authorities on boundaries, Dr. Henry Cloud, who has co-authored more than 20 books on the topic, and success-fully maintained two practices—one in private practice psychology, and one as a top leadership coach. I'd say that he knows a thing or two about the practical application of boundaries. He says the following:

> "Boundary construction is most evident in three-year-olds. By this time, they should have mastered the following tasks:
>
> 1. The ability to be emotionally attached to others, yet without giving up a sense of self and one's freedom to be apart,
>
> 2. The ability to say appropriate no's to others without fear of loss of love,
>
> 3. The ability to take appropriate no's from others without withdrawing emotionally.
>
> Noting these tasks, a friend said half-joking, 'They need to learn this by age three? How about by forty-three?' Yes, these are tall orders but boundary development is essential in the early years of life."
>
> — Henry Cloud, *Boundaries: When to Say Yes, How to Say No to Take Control of Your Life*[10]

These three tasks seem a little overwhelming, am I right? The capture the flag game demonstrates this, but what happens when the field is full of red flags? And how do we navigate this in the domains of our own lives?

Impostor Syndrome and Boundaries

I've always had to work hard to see success. I've had to work through developing plans, backup plans, and third string plans because I've viewed failure of a plan as a failure against me—and the achiever in me won't tolerate failures. As a result, I developed a nasty habit of "doing it myself" for a long time. I've worked with and led teams with great capacity and have experienced the thrill of joint successes, as well as the pain of a team failure. Perhaps you're like me in this way—a shared success is everybody's success, but a team failure is a reflection of me, their leader. It is a heavy burden to bear, and I believe it is closely related to not cultivating a healthy system of boundaries, expectations, and checkups along the way. When we rush into the pursuit of excellence without a proper understanding of the cost of sustainability, all sorts of things can become obstacles.

A thread that I recognized early in my career, which has continued to this day, is the fear that I don't have what it takes to make it in the business (no matter what business it was). That when success was coming, my lack of skill, talent, knowledge, depth, acumen, you name it, would be discovered and I would be promptly shut out on my ear. It feels like it is easier to let a woman go, even if that's not true, but I suspect that it might be the remnants of patriarchal societal expectations still lingering around. You know, the one that places the woman in the kitchen, or behind the secretary desk, or, if she must, as a teacher or nurse. While these are all fine roles and responsibilities, some women are just made for different challenges. I was very aware of some of these expectations and remnants, and because I'm driven to succeed and impress, it caused me to put in more effort, more time, and more of myself than perhaps was healthy. It also was an excellent breeding ground for resentment and resistance to change. The harder the hill became to climb, the deeper I dug in my heels.

Interestingly, as I write this, I see some resonance in my personal relationships (friendships, romantic, and professional partnerships). Doing more has always been an area of comfort for me, but the companionship of resentment is not welcomed.

Now, more than ever before, I am grateful for the work of Pauline Rose Clance and Suzanne Imes. In that groundbreaking work previously mentioned, "The Impostor Phenomenon in High Achieving Women: Dynamics and Therapeutic Intervention", they get to the heart of their research and explain how their interviews echoed much of the same struggle that women were confessing:

The fear that "my stupidity will be discovered" is constantly present; consequently the woman studies or works very hard to prevent the discovery. Hard work and study pay off in excellent performance and approval from authorities. The cycle, worry about intelligence—hard work and cover-up strategies—good grades or performance—approval and temporary good feelings, is reinforcing. The woman feels elated temporarily and such feelings of success make the cycle very hard to give up. She develops an unstated but vaguely aware belief that if she were to think she could succeed she would actually fail. Her belief takes on the quality of a magical ritual, which will guarantee at least an overt success. However, the success is an empty one, and the good feelings are short lived because the underlying sense of phoniness remains untouched.[1]

Is this a red flag for you? How has it manifested in your personal and professional life?

Positivity Versus Naivety

As a lifelong optimist, knowing what to do when I've become a collector of red flags is not necessarily my strength. In fact, I have, over and over again in work environments and personally, captured the red flags and held on to them, failing to share them and release them. I've been a red flag collector. One of the red flags that I've collected, or navigated, over the years has been related to bosses. Not horrible bosses, but giving the benefit of the doubt to the leader I follow to a fault. In the 20 years of my professional career, I've only had two female bosses! And one of the two reported to a man, who was responsible for all things related to our work, so essentially, *he* was the leader I followed.

Why do I think it is important to bring this up? In our society, men are seen as providers, and women are often seen as nurturers. When we support those perceptions, it's harder to maintain boundaries. We juggle so many things so that someone else can shine. We write off the red flags because we don't have a free hand left to grab them!

I've already confessed that my struggle with professional boundaries was related to my battle with impostor syndrome, so now, confession number two: I'm a people pleaser. I grew up as the youngest in my family, have always been outgoing and rather entertaining, and truly love making people feel good. Great on a Saturday evening for dinner, terrible on a Thursday staff meeting when BossMan has a list of things that no one is delivering on and getting frustrated. I know from personal experience that when working with an underperforming staff, following a (usually male) leader who I've been devoted to, I've put myself out there to perform tasks "for the sake of the team" that others wouldn't or couldn't do, in my opinion. I'd like to say that unselfish team effort swells the waves and rises the tide for everyone, but that's usually not the case. When it's not, there's usually room on the shore for resentment. Red flag!

One of the hazards of positivity is that others sometimes regard the positive person as naive. Another hazard of this disposition is that positivity sometimes covers up other things, like insecurity, fear, and a false humility narrative.

Be aware of this cycle, and look for some of your own personal red flags. When you're about to burn out, what are the physical and emotional triggers you should be looking out for? Some common indicators of stress to the max that are sometimes written off:

- Increased alcohol or prescription drug usage
- More frequent feelings of anger, irritability, or anxiety
- Depression
- Hair loss, weight loss, or weight gain in short periods of time
- Restlessness
- Difficulty sleeping, or an increase in sleepiness
- Nagging worry or racing thoughts
- Memory or concentration difficulty
- Making erratic or poor decisions, which is out of character

Getting honest about these red flags is part of stepping into the light, by starting to establish boundaries and heal. The physical red flags are more obvious than those relational red flags, that's for sure. Everyone notices the clothes not fitting and the clump of hair in the shower, but how many people are aware of the shortness and irritation they are meeting people with? Many women instinctively put themselves in the service of others—getting coffee, arranging meals and meetings, taking notes, and making difficult calls. In an exploration of the motivations behind the actions, one might pick up on some of those relational red flags.

Relational Red Flags

At the heart of a woman is a longing to be seen, to be loved, and to be rescued. In the best circumstances, it avails her to a kind of vulnerability that brings out the best in those around her. In the worst circumstances, it unveils particular weaknesses that are subject to exploitation. Colette Dowling[11] coined the term "Cinderella complex", which describes an unconscious desire to be taken care of by others. The hell with that. I am very aware of the fact that I would *love* to be taken care of from time to time. But, as a woman, a working wife and mother, I do most of the caretaking. Why? Well, perhaps it's my own sense of empathy and compassion, perhaps it's my own perfectionist tendencies, and perhaps it's just because, at the end of the day, for she who leads, everyone gets served. Sometimes this shows up and looks like the model employee, the volunteer, the dutiful wife/mother/daughter/sister/niece, or the permanent chairperson. Whatever you call it, when the inability to say "no" suffocates the ability to say "yes", there's a relational white flag waiting to be waved. The inability to say "no" might trigger something that looks like a giving and generous person, but really it's because she is looking for someone to do the same thing for her. The relational red flags to look for here are the twinges of resentment she feels at serving her family or clients. The relational red flags might also show up as envy, jealousy, or anger when viewing other women (or social media images of other women's lifestyles). The relational red flags might *also* look like withdrawal from relationships and intimacy. These red flags are good for giving insight to how other people might see you, going far beyond the Cinderella complex. These red flags are good indicator that it might be time to wave the white flag and surrender to some solitude.

Environmental Red Flags

Just like the red, puffy eyes and runny nose are clear indicators that allergens are in the air outside every spring, sleepless nights, changes in appetite, and digestive issues are usually indicators that there's something that needs your attention. Perhaps easier to identify and accept, as they are usually something happening to someone else, giving insight to a culture issue that isn't quite right. These are the environmental red flags, the things we witness, spurring us either to step aside, step away, or step into the line of fire. The environmental red flags trigger our fight or flight response, narrowing down the pathways in our brains to just two choices: get into it, or get out.

The environmental red flags might be more common and identifiable in some industries—identified as sexism, ageism, racism, or any of the other "isms" that negatively impact progress.

Many women in leadership roles are inclined to step in, but unfortunately may not have the right tools at their disposal, haven't honed their own strengths, or are so guided by empathy that, while they experience the sensation of identifying a red flag, they aren't able to activate a protest or objection in a way that makes change happen. This causes additional stress, and we all know what happens when stress enters the picture. These red flags make for a most unpleasant work environment, a stressful home environment, and a fatigued health environment. Let's take a look at a few of those red flags environmentally:

• **Corporate (or Organizational) Culture** As thought leader, author, and business she-ro Neysha Arcelay speaks to a crowd of executive-level networkers about diversity, we could nearly hear a pin drop because talking about workplace culture is never comfortable. Too many people have a little bit of guilt to pass around, along with the buck, because most organizations struggle to be as open-minded as they claim to be. Neysha offers this perspective: "A healthy culture pursues a common purpose through achievable yet challenging goals and fosters diversity of thought, collaboration, transformation, authenticity, and accountability." When an organization permits or promotes a culture that is destructive to the dignity of the human person, something in a woman's (or person's) heart responds. The subtle (or not so subtle) chiseling away at our being has a deep impact. Our motivation wanes, our respect for the organization is fractured, and our view changes. It's one thing to have corporate values printed and framed; it's another thing to put them into action. When words have no meaning, the organizational culture has no weight. Sadly, many of us have been on the other side and felt the negativity that comes from a poor commitment to organizational values and an unhealthy work culture. This drives us, in droves, out of the traditional work environment and into something...else.

- **Expectations of Pace and Consistency in Performance or Scheduling** In a global economy, we are expected to always be available to clients. In a digital world, we are expected to always be responsive to our colleagues and superiors. In a virtual reality, the perception of success is more important than contentment. This is the world we are living in. This is where the glorification of busy is triumphant. This is where the pace and consistency of work and life is put into hyperspeed and few people speak up to stop it, or slow it down. When the bar is constantly moving, it's difficult to know when enough is enough. For women especially, there's a standard of performance that we are measured against. Especially if we carefully balance caregiving and breadwinning. Especially if we battle commutes or multiple schedules. Or travel. Or sell. Or anything else at all, because let's be honest, even though women are closing the wage gap for paid services, we still carry a whole hell of a lot of unpaid duties in a wildly disproportionate rate to our male counterparts. These expectations drive us to (drink or) burn out.

- **Community (or lack of)** The old adage "it takes a village" might still be true in theory, but is certainly untrue in application, and often accessibility. It doesn't change the need for relationships, support, and community. Our digitally connected workplaces and relationships have, in one sense, made it easier to keep in touch and know what others are in to, but at the same time has made it more difficult to cultivate deep, authentic relationships. Women especially have never been more alone. When our deepest longing is to be known, our greatest pain is in being alone. The isolation experienced by women who are striving to do it all, be it all, and have it all is greater than anyone would ever have guessed, if they weren't walking around in our (mostly uncomfortable) classic pumps. When we need a friend, we can easily find a Netflix binge, bottle of Pinot, or a pint of ice cream. What we really need is a friend—the kind of friend who will hand you toilet paper under the stalls in the ladies' restroom. That kind of community is hard to find, unless, of course, you're in the ladies' restroom. For some reason, we're all at our best in there.

- **The Breakdown of Healthy Communication** I recently learned that American workers are engaged in nearly three hours of conflict at work each week. This translates into 150 hours a year. It looks like protecting turf (real and relational), sounds like gossip and sarcasm, and it hurts production, profits, and people. While there are corporate cultures that approach conflict in healthy ways and create an environment around honesty and organizational health, cultivating an awareness of those professional red flags and inconsistencies may give insight to greater integrity issues in the business, which is always helpful.

I tend to be an eternal optimist. I see the best in people first. I ignore red flags—we've already established that, right? When I first left my long tenure in the non-profit space, I saw every person in business as amazing, and smarter, stronger, and more successful than I felt. I trusted my leaders and boss, and found myself writing excuses for an inappropriate comment here, a tasteless remark there. It began with strangers, then it became comments about clients, and although I wasn't comfortable, I wasn't going to stir the pot. This growing awareness of broken promises, disparaging remarks, and failure to follow through ultimately led to a separation from the company. Unfortunately for me, I wasn't surprised at all when that separation opened the door to more broken promises (of payments), disparaging remarks (to friends and clients), and a failure to follow through with contractual obligations. I learned the hard way that communication red flags are always external indicators of an individual's interior disposition.

Sometimes we struggle with communicating intentions and frustrations, and that's understandable. Many women were raised to believe that "good little girls are to be seen and not heard", and that when a woman speaks up, she's a bitch. Unfortunately for all of us, the biases against women who speak the truth will continue far beyond our lifespans. The gender bias is real, and we aren't going to change it universally, but we can do our part to change it in our own workplaces and relationships by harnessing self-control and clearheadedness when facing conflict. For she who leads, running from conflict isn't an option. Nor is stomping our feet and screaming. For she who leads, firming our steps and steadying our chins is necessary for communicating in all ways that we have something important to contribute and we will be making that known.

Finally, communicating our position is squarely our responsibility. Receiving and acting on the information is the responsibility of the other. Communication red flags that show up based on a lack of responsibility are more concerning than those which show up as a result of a lack of understanding. We can work through understanding, but resistance to change or communication is a red flag that is much tougher to put down.

For she who leads, the environmental red flags are not to be taken lightly. These environmental red flags might be just the thing to trigger something bigger—a health episode, a financial downturn, a reputation capsizing, or just a really stressful and negative experience.

We have the greatest level of control over the relational red flags, and we have the least control over environmental red flags. It is possible to establish healthy and appropriate boundaries as a method for controlling professional red flags, but that isn't easy. Setting up boundaries and outlining your non-negotiables needs to happen before entering into a situation, and with a clear understanding of the impacts on all parts of the system. (More on that in Chapter 9, "Applying the Stuff".)

Discussion/Reflection Questions

What are some of the boundaries that would maintain harmony in your home/work life? To help you get started, let's think about some of these basics:

• Time away from family/occupied with professional pursuit

• Acceptable/unacceptable behaviors for self/others

• Lines that will not be crossed by you/against you

Can you think of a time when a boundary was crossed that negatively impacted you? What happened and what did you learn?

What is one thing that you can do to begin securing boundaries for your next steps?

"Boundaries define us. They define what is me and what is not me. A boundary shows me where I end and someone else begins, leading me to a sense of ownership. Knowing what I am to own and take responsibility for gives me freedom. Taking responsibility for my life opens up many different options. Boundaries help us keep the good in and the bad out. Setting boundaries inevitably involves taking responsibility for your choices. You are the one who makes them. You are the one who must live with their consequences. And you are the one who may be keeping yourself from making the choices you could be happy with. We must own our own thoughts and clarify distorted thinking."

— Henry Cloud, *Boundaries: When to Say Yes, How to Say No, to Take Control of Your Life*[10]

Chapter 3

Values Trump Preferences

Remember when we were kids, and we first discovered an alternate use for a deck of playing cards? Building a structure by carefully leaning each card upon another layer by layer, reaching new heights with a steady hand. Until a door opens, or an older sibling leans in and blows it over. When we waffle and bend to please others or avoid offending anyone, our choices have the strength of that deck of playing cards stacked up by a screen door. When we know what we are about, we have the power and ability to adapt and do brave things. The brave thing is seldom the easy thing, the cost-effective thing, the comfortable thing. Doing the right thing matters. Well, let's be honest, everything matters.

I have a friend who shared a story with me about finding herself at the top of a house of cards professionally. A female in a very male-driven industry. A female top performer in a room full of men who didn't think too much about the women they worked with, sold to, or were married to. A female who had heard enough. When one of her direct reports was the topic of conversation, the house of cards was about to blow over.

There's the old adage, popular in social studies classrooms in the '90s: "You've got to stand for something, or you'll fall for anything". Being guided by the core belief that people are important, and that some things are never right, is important. When a person (or company) proclaims one thing, and executes another, we question their integrity. For men and for women in business, in relationships, and interiorally, integrity matters much more than the number in our bank account, zip code, or real estate square footage. When the external things get more attention than the internal things, you can be sure that something is going to fall apart.

So what are values?

How do they guide us?

And what happens when we aren't sure about what we stand for?

Values are the ideas and ideals that an individual will base decisions upon. They may change at some point, but usually they have a longer shelf life than emotions and feelings. If values are like oatmeal, emotions are like cereal. They fill us up and give us what we need, and both can be very messy when knocked over or ignored for a while. Have you ever found a forgotten bowl of Cheerios after a week or so? *Gross!* Crusty, stale little mounds and flaky, sour milk. A little thing creates a big mess when not dealt with properly.

Values are *not* universal. Just because something is important to you doesn't mean it is guaranteed to be important to somebody else. Values *can* guide us, but that's only if we have either 1) a strong resolve, 2) a goal which aligns with our values, or 3) an environment that is harmonious with our values. We get into conflict when our values do not align with the relationships, responsibilities, and reality that we are situated in. That's where choice comes in. And sisters, that is some tough stuff right there.

I have a number of friends and clients who have achieved remarkable success—beautiful women in their forties working in companies, industries, and roles that require them to be superwomen. Women of virtue with known values, who have had to fight, claw, tear, and creep along for every advancement they achieved. I also know incredible women with beautiful hearts and terrific minds who have compromised their values and dealt with the internal disappointment and conflict as a result. It's tough, no matter where you sit on this seesaw. The reality is that institutional behaviors influence the cultural norms that many of us operate in, and they don't give a rip whether or not there is value alignment. That's why it is so critically important for our long-term satisfaction that we spend time establishing values and guiding behaviors for ourselves. Take the time to discover, rediscover, and discuss that which guides you.

Values trump preferences every day of the week, if you know what you're working with.

In my work as a certified professional behavior analyst, I've discovered that people's behaviors are largely driven by their preferences. For more dominant personalities, preferences are boldly proclaimed and in their weakest moments may manifest as haughtiness, boorishness, or aggressiveness. For more submissive personalities, core motivation shows up and in weakened moments these behavior preferences manifest as pacifism, martyrdom, or passive-aggressiveness, to name a few. In our best, most self-aware states, the behaviors and preferences associated with them allow us to harness our gifts and power to do difficult things. But when we are feeling threatened or weak, the dark side of preferences peeks through. Preferences in themselves are objective and good; it's only when we seek to alter reality to accommodate our preferences and make others subject to our feelings that we find conflict. Feelings are another F-word that can get us off track, especially as women who are already being scrutinized and judged. Like food, it has its value and validity, but it also can't be overused or left to run wild.

For she who leads, behaviors have to be rooted in something more than the moment.

·········· **THINK IT OUT** ··········

Discussion/Reflection Questions

Values

Take a stab at it. Name and define three values that guide you in your behaviors and decision making.

Value: _____, defined as

Value: _____, defined as

Value: _____, defined as

Behaviors

How do you feel when you see injustice around you?

What are the injustices that stir the most inside you? OR Bias check.

What's one thing you have the power to do in these situations?

"Always *do right*. This will gratify some people
and astonish the rest."

— Mark Twain[12]

CHAPTER 4

Vision and Decision Making

The ability to use reason, logic, and intellect in our leadership is powerful. The woman who leads herself, others, and her organization through industry, passion and "thought leadership" must communicate her message powerfully as well.

I remember meeting Tina when I was a young woman, working in non-profit. Not the "I work in an office all day" kind of non-profit. I was in the grit of it, the jeans and t-shirt non-profit space. I was a hustler, so I carried a part-time (and sometimes full-time) job in addition to my non-profit work. My values were clear—I wanted to be in this role and contributing as I was—but my budget didn't like it, so I supplemented.

Tina was beautiful, professional, a "boss babe" in every sense of the word. I met her because my high school best friend and post-college graduate roommate worked with her at a search firm in the greater Pittsburgh area. Tina was hosting a happy hour for clients, or prospects, or people with "grown-up" jobs. I wouldn't have identified myself as having a "grown-up" job, but heck, I was there for the free appetizers (budget friendly).

When Tina was introduced to me, she treated me like I belonged there. As if I was someone worthy of socializing at this business function. I was not a future client. I was not a profit. She could gain nothing from me. And yet she treated me as though I belonged, spoke to me like I was important, and welcomed me in a way that cannot be manufactured. I was kind of amazed. Yes, this kind of integrity is amazing and compelling. But you have to know more about Tina to understand why her brand of leadership is so impactful.

Tina's early career was spent in the life sciences and healthcare industries. She liked to work, so she navigated her way through operations, customer service, and sales roles at a global leader in the allergy vaccination space. Subsequently, she was able to advance into training and sales roles for another six years with one of the world's largest clinical laboratories. After a couple of life-changing developments (having children) and a cross-country move, Tina spent the next decade of her career in the search industry, working for two of the largest executive search firms in the country (and perhaps even the world, depending on who you talk to). Tina kept moving up, and on to the next thing. When I met Tina, she was already impressive. I'm forever grateful for the way that she mentored me and challenged me to think about the investment of my immediate next steps in relation to my ultimate goals, values, and future.

Something that bears repeating, especially in the search industry, is that not all recruiters are equal. Not all firms do business ethically. Not all professionals behave professionally. I learned this the hard way, but not from Tina. Like I said, when I met Tina, I had nothing that she wanted or needed to achieve the next level of success. I was just a kid in ripped jeans trying to be a grown-up in a grown-up world. What I saw in the search industry was that people weren't always treated with respect. Sometimes they are seen as commodities—a means to an end for landing the right candidate for a client so that they could get paid. Tina, however, saw things much differently. She follows some simple principles: 1) There are no wasted conversations. 2) Be honest as soon as you know someone is not the right fit. Don't string people along. 3) Follow up with everyone.

Observing Tina over the years, and seeking her for counsel, had a big impact on me personally.

As a professional mentor, she passed those three principles on to me, and reinforced them with her actions. Tina was also famous for saying that she was "reserving the right to get smarter". I even talked about Tina during an interview when I was leaving my 15-year career in the non-profit space and daring to step out into something completely new and different. I was a little nervous, but I knew that I could apply my values of respecting people to a vision for success.

She stepped out of her big firm and launched an operation of her own, doing things her way, and seeking out a partner that was aligned with her vision. Tina's courage, coupled with hard work, fed her vision for what the industry needed and she became a guiding light for her clients, peers, and partners. When I finally had the opportunity to work with her, the principles were still there. They hadn't changed and the hard work that we were all accustomed to allowed us to make some decisions with clearly aligned vision, not frustration or fear.

Courage, coupled with hard work, is baked into our DNA as woman. Turning to science, we can examine the growing slab of research tracing the biological composition of women's brains. We really are wired differently than our male counterparts. And it starts at a very early age. The phenomenon of the female brain gives us a superpower—we are able to pull together pieces of information that shape our decisions differently. It's not just the information placed before us that allows us to make decisions—we are accessing details, memories, observations, feelings, and experiences creating an ability to see the big picture, not only the page. Stanford researches conducted and published a study in 2017 outlining this, saying, "Discoveries like this one should ring researchers' alarm buzzers. Women, it's known, retain stronger, more vivid memories of emotional events than men do. They recall emotional memories more quickly, and the ones they recall are richer and more intense. If, as is likely, the amygdala figures into depression or anxiety, any failure to separately analyze men's and women's brains to understand their different susceptibilities to either syndrome would be as self-defeating as not knowing left from right. The two hemispheres of a woman's brain talk to each other more than a man's do."[13]

Naturally, this would indicate that behavior differences show up. Women, it seems, are pre-wired to work smarter, not harder. This can be a value to guide you, too. If it's "what you see is what you get", then get your eye on the BIG picture. See the whole thing, and then pay attention to the details. Smart people make S.M.A.R.T. goals to help them achieve that success. What might a S.M.A.R.T. goal look like for you?

Specific

Measurable

Attainable

Realistic or Relevant

Timebound

A good example of a S.M.A.R.T. goal is: *I will spend 15 minutes each day in silence and meditation while I am driving home from work.*

It's S.M.A.R.T. because it's:

Specific: 15 minutes, driving in silence, meditating

Measurable: 15 minutes, each day. You either DID it, or DIDN'T do it.

Attainable: Attainable if commute is 15 minutes!

Realistic or Relevant: Seems like a doable goal, not outside of your realm of control under most circumstances (unless you carpool...)

Timebound : 15 minutes, 5 days a week. I might suggest adding for 30, 60, or 90 days as well, so that you can track the goal.

Some other metrics can go along with a S.M.A.R.T. goal like that. Checking blood pressure weekly, for example, might make sense. Meditation is known for stress reduction. Perhaps another metric to accompany that particular goal would be responsiveness: how are your emotions and reactions to situations which would normally set you off? Think about what metrics might accompany your own S.M.A.R.T. goal and write it down.

"I'm not getting criticized at home *any* more!" This is *not* a S.M.A.R.T. goal. With a situation like this, you probably don't have a whole lot of control about what another person lays upon you. You do have choices though. Your response to an external stimulus can give you control over your emotions, reactions, and experiences. Boundaries matter, my friends. And, more often than not, creating a discipline around establishing and maintaining boundaries conditions us with the grit we need to effectively manage ourselves through difficult situations. Women are biologically conditioned to do hard things.

Tina's vision was clear: create something better, different, and meaningful in the search industry. Reserve the right to get better, and constantly redefine the process. Her brand was clear, she was a winner. Her leadership was evident, she invested in others. Her partnership was authentic, she met everyone with that openness. For she who leads like Tina, courage comes with activating the vision and applying it to decision making.

Discussion/Reflection Questions

When have you had to access your grit and grace in order to make the impossible possible?

What is one thing you would like to do, see through, or accomplish in the next year that will require more?

What steps will you need to take to achieve that one thing?

SOMETHING TO PONDER

"It's just as important to know when to drop something and shift direction as it is to know when to stick with something. When we quit the things that aren't working for us, we free up our willpower and perseverance for the things that really do matter."

— Rich Karlgaard, *Late Bloomers: The Power of Patience in a World Obsessed with Early Achievement*[14]

CHAPTER 5

Failure, Fear and Frustration: Do More, Not Less

I grew up on a farm. I was ashamed of it, growing up, because I thought we were too poor and worked too hard. I wanted neighbors in the worst way, but we lived far off the beaten path. Literally on the other side of the tracks. But the farm was a great place to grow up! We had fields of corn and potatoes, green beans, pear trees, and apple trees. In the middle of the main vegetable garden, there was this fantastic raspberry bush that my brother and I would run into and hide. One time, he ran into the bush, encountered the angry side of a swarm of bees, and my larger-than-life father picked him up and threw him in the pool. He survived without anaphylaxis and we cut back that bush a great deal for the following year. Although I grew up on a farm, I never quite learned how to keep a garden weed free, prune a bush, or maintain a harvest. But those years of shucking corn in the back of a pickup truck on the side of the road or in the bank parking lot, using my little hands and "nimble fingers" as my dad put it, served a good purpose. Apparently, peeling away is easier than weeding and pruning, but it would take me more than 20 years to learn that.

Because I was the youngest, I didn't always have to do the same kind of work that my siblings were responsible for. And because of that, most summers, I was lonely. I had plenty of animals to talk to, and could always help my mom inside the house, but even there, the housework, didn't produce the same kind of results that the outdoor work did. We weren't making anything besides beds, and we weren't producing anything besides piles of clean laundry, only to be soiled again. At an early age I already understood the invisibility that so many women feel as they lovingly and dutifully tend to the household responsibilities. Even then, I felt like I needed to do something to earn the same kind of love, attention, and praise that my older siblings might have gotten. I was longing for the experience of being seen, being known, and being important. The connection that I needed (and still need) is rooted in relationship. As a young girl living on a farm in the middle of nowhere, I really wanted a friend. I longed for someone to talk to and share secrets with. I made friends in school, and some friends were fascinated with the farm. Some friends weren't. I think that I may have gotten set up for lifelong disappointment in those early years—thinking the I had to perform, impress, and maintain an appearance in order to be really worthy of friendship. If I wasn't *doing* something, was I doing it wrong?

A familiar thread that I've seen show up in myself, and in the relationships that I hold dearest to me, is the "do more, not less" expression of love. I'd love to say that I completely understand this motivation, but I can tell you this: as an achiever, I want to be doing more. I value the relationships and connections in my life, and I have no problem going deep with strangers. I exchange compliments in the supermarket. I exchange business cards on airplanes. I meet a stranger once and they become a friend. I become more by giving more. I want to be pouring in to the people who are important to me. And I don't think that I should be apologetic or ashamed of the fact that I do love people hard. But if you love like this, it is going to hurt. For she who leads with love, failure, fear, and frustration will threaten to puncture holes in the delicate bags we carry for ourselves and everyone else.

Connection: The Competition Challenge

Female friendships are challenging, are they not? We aren't all the same, and our methods and means of communicating vary quite a bit. Relationships change, and even in the early years, as females play together and relationally challenge each other, we are learning patterns of behavior which often stick with us. These early relationships help us to navigate other relationships—turning into partnerships, competitive relationships, professional relationships, mentoring relationships, and even romantic relationships. What we learn about relating to others starts early. And understanding what healthy relationships should look like is critical, but not easy. The breakdown in female friendships can be more painful than a breakup in a romantic relationship. There's a competition challenge that exists among many women, especially since we relate who we are with a notion of "whose we are". Women often respond to basic introductory questions by explaining the relationships in their life: "Kevin's wife", "I have two sons", "I take care of...". Little by little, it's almost like our own identity erodes into a position of service and relationship, and many of us are glad to give ourselves away. Yet, there's a competition challenge in that, because for us, managing these relationships has a way of keeping score internally and often unintentionally. Deborah Tannen has researched and written extensively on this subject, and explores the relationships between men and women, and between women and their friends, peers, and sisters. She says, "Women are simply competitive in a way that's less obvious—they're competitive about connection." Connection. The one thing many of us want, but none of us can fake.

Because I love big, I hurt big too. Perhaps you have similar experiences to me, in that you've had friendships disappoint you. Perhaps you're a forgiver too, and your heart gets broken. There's a fear of getting hurt that can linger, sneak in, and then cause a person to become jaded and safely tucked away from the threat of intimacy with others. Intimacy certainly requires a vulnerability, but the alternative is closing off connection and sitting in isolation. There have been times when I've waited too long to reach out, allowing silence to speak volumes and tell a story that I didn't believe. There have been times that I've spoken too soon and said things I didn't mean. Managing ourselves in moments of changing connections, pain, and intense vulnerability can only happen when we understand what is happening and sincerely try to stop reacting.

Changing the Connection

The difference between annual plants and perennials is that an annual plant has a life cycle that lasts only one year. Plant. Water. Feed. Grow. Bloom. Die. Perennials have a different root system. They grow, bloom, and appear to die. Then they return in the next spring and repeat the cycle. I grew up on a farm and honest to God I have to look it up every time I see these words on a package and cannot, for the life of me, tell the difference when I see a plant. I just plant seeds, hope for the best, and am pleasantly surprised if something else shows up a year later! (My sister, on the other hand, has an incredible gift for growing, tending to, identifying, and greenkeeping. I did not inherit those genes.) True to form, my experience of managing relationships greatly mirrors the way I manage a garden. Plant seeds. Water them. Feed them. Keep up with weeds for a bit. Harvest. Wonder if it will die or just go dormant. Pleasantly surprised by another bloom. Hang on to frozen pots all winter, not sure if it is an annual or perennial. Ask my husband about the collection of buckets of dirt we are keeping.

As people change, relationships change. As relationships change, we need to change our expectations of the other person. This is hard, hard work. Sometimes backing away from a friendship or professional relationship for a season is best for everyone. Sometimes getting in the weeds and figuring out which root system goes where is the work to be done. I'm hesitant to weed out relationships in my life, and I know this, because I was so lonely in my earliest years. I tend to hang on to people for a long time, wishing for the best, and hoping that things work out. I let friends back in, I give second chances, and I forgive. It doesn't always work out, and I'm aware of that. But that's the essence of the "do more" that my heart was made for. I've leveraged the usage of boundaries (as discussed in Chapter 2) to help protect myself, my business, and my family from an overuse of this "do more"-ness. Understanding which relationships are annual and which are perennial helps to let the right things go when the circumstances and connection are wrong.

Some connections break. Some relationships fail. Some people don't want to be in your life. Some relationships slip into dormancy. Some relationships need to be done. It's okay to acknowledge that. For she who leads, recognizing the difference between dormant and done is important for our own growth.

Deaths

One of my closest friends throughout college and my twenties suddenly, unexpectedly, and tragically passed away, leaving behind a husband and children. I was about to get married, and I had been in her wedding and we had shared so much of our lives. We had fallen out a year or two earlier, gotten busy, and never mended things. Her death was one of the biggest blows in my 38 years of life. I never thought that our friendship was done. I never imagined not sharing my own family with her, in the way that she shared her family with me. I had a lot of things left unspoken when I attended her funeral. The truth about life and relationships is that you may never get closure. You might not have the chance to see things through to an ending at all, because endings show up sometimes before we are ready. For she who leads, being honest about endings builds endurance.

Death comes at us in ways that we really can't be ready for. The finality of it all. Whether this is an actual death, the closure of a business, the loss of a home, or the ending of a marriage, we, as women, aren't always as gentle with ourselves or with others when there are endings that we *think* could have been avoided. It's impossible to fully understand how a person (or a couple) get to the point of ending. The truth is, sometimes bankruptcy is the only thing left to do. Sometimes foreclosure is the only thing left to do. Sometimes divorce is the only thing left to do. The truth is, none of these things are contagious, so when fear is the primary motivator to do less and back away, we can fight this with mighty hearts who do more. For she who leads, resisting fear as a motivator makes us stronger.

Frustration Is Also a Function

While I admittedly am a "do more" person, sometimes doing more for yourself in a kind and respectful way is healthiest. Taking that time to reflect. Stepping back out of an exhausting social situation. Becoming unavailable when a friendship becomes draining. Loosening some of the emotional ties and connections when a marriage is beating you down. So how do you know when it is time to take a breather or when it is time to quit? I mean, really call it quits on a dream, a project, or a vocational plan? And is it really a failure to decide that something dead needs to be buried?

It's okay to step back from a friendship, marriage, or professional relationship if you've exhausted reasonable means for maintenance and healing. No one deserves to be a doormat. It's not a failure. Can you objectively identify root causes and circumstances for the situation as it is presently? Are you hanging on to the past without managing the emotions around it? Can you move yourself (and those you are responsible for) forward without failure, fear, and frustration negatively impacting your ability to freely choose a next step? This is a time to do more, not less. Failure shows up when we quit before we've made peace with our decisions. Making peace with our decisions comes from an objective evaluation of the real motivations for the choices we make. We are free to make any choice we wish, but we are not free from the consequences. Do more, where you can, and experience the freedom of a heart motivated by honesty about connections, needs, and frustrations. For she who leads with heart, there's really no fear of failure.

Discussion/Reflection Questions

How has letting go of something you loved so much changed you?

Where have fear, frustration, and failure gotten you?

Describe some of the friendships that have helped you to walk through fires

SOMETHING TO PONDER

"Be who God meant you to be and you
will set the world on fire."

— St. Catherine of Siena[15]

CHAPTER 6

Time for a Time Out

There is this lie that exists—the one that says that as women, we should expect to have it all, be expected to do it all, and deserve whatever we want for being all things to all people. Okay, maybe that's a couple of lies all compounded into one giant "WHAT THE HELL AM I DOING?!" I need to say this, and I do say this, over and over and over again. It is a lie. As a young(ish) working wife and mother, I struggled under the pressure of my work and the commute and the responsibilities of all the things that I valued and defined my success (self-worth) by. I struggled so much that I caved. First, I took a sabbatical. It was really an extended maternity leave that left me feeling even more angsty than when I started. Then I switched jobs. Then I switched jobs again. Each step took me a little further away from the frying pan that I felt that I was in, and dangled my extremities a little more over the fire. I replaced one stress with another. I swapped out one self-imposed expectation for a different one. I didn't think I could do anything well, and felt like I had lost a little of myself in the process. What was going on?

Thanks to growing bodies of research and attention given to the stress levels of working moms, and motherhood in general, words like "anxiety" and "depression" come up in more conversations, and Google searches, than ever before. A growing body of research had some of the answers I was looking for. My days and nights were being dedicated to caring for and raising children. My professional drive was causing me to push limits and perform. My instincts were steering much of the ship, but I was pushing practicality aside and burning the candle at both ends. At work and at home, I was beat.

Motherhood and Apple Pie

I can't. I can't. I can't.

It's not working. I'm not working. This isn't working.

The track of frustrations was playing on and on in my head when I stepped out into a new career, and I was stuck. My mentor leaned in to me and said something like, "I know you're frustrated. But this will come to you like motherhood and apple pie." I remember looking straight ahead and thinking "oh, shit", because I am literally the worst at both motherhood *and* apple pie. We all know what struggles a mom goes through as she works to get the hang of growing, raising, and keeping a tiny human alive...and most of us have experienced the disaster of pie making. This isn't going to be good.

When I thought about why that phrase didn't settle my tormented soul (drama added naturally—you're welcome), I realized that there's good reason for this. I am an achiever. An activator. A strategist. I find ways to create things. Build things. Fix things. Professionally, I get to get up every day and use each one of my signature strengths to be the architect of my career, the author of my success, and the determiner of my boundaries. As a well-educated and driven boss babe, I knew that I had capacity, capabilities, and options. It was all about balance for me. I was stressed. Frustrated. Feeling guilty all the time. I needed to step away from what I knew and look for something better. Did I have the right ingredients?

For me, the role didn't matter. People excited me. I worked in a boutique firm, constantly redefining priorities and services. It should have been perfect for a working mother—enough flexibility to parent, enough challenges to never be bored. Prior to all of this, I spent years in a leadership role in a huge organization, but it didn't quite fill this need that I had to develop people whole-person, not just performing functions. In my early career, I dedicated years to developing others—I was made to be a coach. I also pounded on doors to get them to open up enough for opportunities to become within reach for the communities and populations I was serving. I truly did love working hard, and I still do. I enjoyed giving more, going further, and bringing others along. For she who leads like me, bless your heart. Burnout is right around the corner, waiting for you to trip in those fabulously appointed heels and wide-leg dress pants.

Career success, options, and opportunities were there for me. I was proud of my accomplishments and nearly defined myself by them. Until the realization of another dream of mine was on the horizon. Starting a family had always been on my mind. When I met and married my husband, who happens to be adopted, I really wanted to give him a child; "someone with his DNA" I always said. It sped up my timeline for parenthood, and I was happy for that. Exactly ten months after our wedding, our first son was born. About two years later, the second. And then things got really crazy. My priorities were shifting. My drive for success professionally hadn't changed, but my willingness to sacrifice motherhood to meet the growing demands certainly did. I could keep pushing, keep working, and keep trying, or I could settle in to the stay at home mom gig. Constantly, people asked me if that is what I was going to do next. No offense to those who choose it, but I was offended that people thought that was what I was going to do. I mean, hadn't they seen me crush goals before? The tension I experienced in finding some balance or harmony between the motherhood I had wanted and gotten, and the professional success I was craving, became too much to bear. I threw myself into work and felt guilty all the time. It made no sense to me then, and still doesn't today. How can this be what I, and many other working moms, experience? The choices should really be easy. After all, I had wanted a family for all these years— and now that I had one, was I going to really just work my time away? Or worse, was I going to resent the people I loved because I desired to work? I did the only thing that I knew how to do: work harder, push more, go further outside of what felt natural to me and keep trying.

So yes, I started to doubt myself, and if I was cut out for any of this. There were loads of tears at this point. Back to motherhood and apple pie: I suck at making apple pies. I can cut the apples. I can mix the dough. But...the chilling of the dough to *just* the right temperature...the rolling and rolling and rolling—so tedious. The lattice, come on now. The pre-baking the apple slices—*what?* Forget it. My apple pies look more like an unfortunate glass dish of apple mush and cinnamon.

At some point, the women around me caught wind of my struggle. Through a lot of long walks, late-night text conversations, and video chats with my mom-tribe, I felt like it was okay to confess that I was struggling, failing, drowning. Just letting that out, breaking out of the "keeping it all together" facade, was actually helping me sort through the working mom/stay at home mom tug-of-war. And that's how it clicked for me. I didn't (and still don't) have to choose one over the other. I don't have to fake it. What I needed to do was find some harmony and purpose. The freedom that I experienced when I realized that I didn't have to fit into someone else's cubicle or crib still gives me hope. And it should give you some hope too. But before that sense of freedom, there was a lot of meticulous following of someone else's recipe. And reading of blogs. And listening to podcasts. And crying in the bathroom. Motherhood and apple pie wasn't natural for me. But developing people, and getting behind them, beside them, and looking for obstacles that might trip them up *was* for me.

It's kind of working in motherhood, but definitely working professionally. I have nothing further to offer on apple pie. There's no fun recipe here. Go to Eat'n Park. They have great pies.

My hope for you: that you will create your own recipe for success based on the ingredients you are bringing to the table. That you will recognize that the way you are made is not a mistake and these traits are not setbacks. For she who leads, learning how to harness your strengths and apply them to the work before you will do you well in life, and in business, opening the door for the things you desire most.

Motivated to pursue my own career by design, and use my strengths to solve problems, I pressed on in my own path. I did the entrepreneurial thing for a while, and then I went back into non-profit work because I needed that pace and consistency. I realized that I can be patient with myself. I said this earlier, but my God it bears repeating: the myth of having a work-life balance frustrated me. As a working parent, I felt like I was constantly taking from one box to put in another. And keeping track. And measuring. And feeling guilty when I had success in one area. And getting frustrated. I was already doing KETO and measuring all those damn macros, I couldn't track one more thing. The frustration was real. This also may explain why I wasn't loving the whole apple pie analogy. I haven't had pie in so long...

I've noticed this wasn't just my problem though—more and more people I encountered professionally were experiencing the same thing. We all wanted something more. Don't you? Don't you want something more for yourself and all the other women that keep striving and struggling and succeeding quietly? We have so much to learn from each other.

Having the right ingredients is one thing, but using them as part of the recipe for success is another.

> "A leader needs to know his strengths as a carpenter knows his tools, or as a physician knows the instruments at her disposal. What great leaders have in common is that each truly knows his or her strength—and can call on the right strength at the right time."
>
> — Don Clifton, psychologist and business executive

Discussion/Reflection Questions

What are some of the beliefs you have about your own state of life that might be limiting your ability to be truly satisfied, happy, and harmonious?

Where do you draw strength from when the pressure is building?

What are the ingredients you would add to your own recipe for success?

SOMETHING TO PONDER

"The emotions have been seen as the center of woman's soul. For that reason, emotional formation will have to be centrally placed in woman's formation."

— Edith Stein, philosopher[16]

CHAPTER 7

Restoration and Rejuvenation

Who would have thought that even as the wage disparity between what men and women take home closes the gap, women would still be putting in more unpaid labor hours than men and burning out at high rates? It's almost like women are earning higher degrees and achieving more high responsibility roles than ever before, and still expected to take on the bulk of the childrearing, caretaking, and homemaking. And no one cares. The research shows that the majority of Americans SAY that women should share home responsibilities with their male counterparts and partners, but it's more complicated than that. The behaviors tell a different story. Even in my own home, as a full-time working mother with multiple projects and extracurricular business responsibilities, I battled with myself over sharing household responsibilities with my husband. There are a couple of practical reasons—women see things differently, and do things differently. But there are also those cultural norms that we experience a degree of pressure to adhere to. Women should tend to the kids and the home, and work, and cook, and plan, and be attractive, and care for their spouses, and... all these other external and internal expectations. In reality, I struggled with every step of my married-working-motherhood experience (and I still do). As someone who has always loved working, separating my achiever behaviors from the core responsibilities was tough. Choosing to leave a stable career that I was successful in and endeavor into a few years of rockier water wasn't easy either. But I wanted to be able to have some freedom to give my family the best of me, not the rest of me, until I had better footing as a woman who was/is married and working and mothering. I may have jumped from the frying pan into the fire, but I learned a little about myself along the way, and encountered three amazing women who taught me how to do this "fire dance". This is for the woman who stepped away and came back with something new. The brave women with stories to tell keep me going, make me better, and help me find that bit of bravery that I need to get through the tough days.

Boss Babes Building an Empire

The first woman that I met in my exploration of fire is Shannon—mother, business creator, author. I met her at a coffee shop and it was like magic. We could have stayed there all day. When she handed me a copy of her book *It's About Time*[17], I committed then and there to read it. After all, it was written for people like me, who wanted to "do more of what matters in the time you have". (Confession: I usually read the book after I had put the kids to bed, wearing Crest whitening strips on my teeth, waiting for hair dye to develop, hiding in my master bathroom. The stains and earmarks on the book are proof. This is the extent of my multi-tasking.) Shannon told me, "There is a misconception that women are 'better at multitasking', but I think we're adept at harmonization. We do well understanding the issue, confronting the challenges with strategies and then tactics, and rallying to get 'er done." Shannon loved her corporate job, her team, the work, and the benefits that came with it. But she sensed that something more was waiting for her. I could relate. In Shannon's own words:

> "I truly felt that I could make a bigger impact and help more businesses by taking the experience and education I had living through multiple mergers and acquisitions to market. When I was integrating sales processes and Salesforce.com instances, I couldn't find a playbook or a partner who had a holistic approach to the change management aspect of it. Now, I'm doing great work with great clients and it's so fulfilling! It was incredibly scary, however, facing the fact that I'd have to 'kill to eat,' and that no paycheck would ever be promised. I gave myself a timeline—either this works in six months or it doesn't—and saved up enough cash to cover those six months. I had a Plan B, Plan C, and a 'what would I do if it doesn't work' drop-dead date, and I worked with a coach who helped me to really set 'SMART goals' to ensure my fears were as quelled as possible."

Shannon left her comfortable and secure corporate job and created the company Cloud Adoption Solutions, helping organizations make sense of CRM software and cloud technology through hands-on training and support, creating a totally new pathway for herself and her family. "Making my employees and clients happy is my number one goal; I am constantly asking them for feedback with the specific question: What could I be doing better? We're all in this together and have the same goals, and I want to make sure we're getting there appropriately. Communication, constant communication, is a MUST," Shannon responded when I asked her about how she keeps her eye on what's most important right now. She was a major encourager along the way—encouraging me to step out and work harder, speak up and tell a story, and even to write this book. I love this encourage-ment most: "Anyone who has the drive, the passion, the pull, and a little smidge of insanity can do this, too! Careful planning is the best way to mitigate risk and future-proof your challenges, so really take the time to avoid the impulse to just jump without first outlining the steps."

Shannon quickly introduced me to Neysha Arcelay, the founder of Precixa, another Pittsburgh-based consulting firm that specializes in the design and delivery of transformative organizational strategies for midsize to large businesses. Prior to starting Precixa, Neysha's talents were being used in impressive ways with impressive companies. But she was balancing incredible talents with the incredible gift of motherhood. While she wasn't ready to step out of the workforce, she was ready to design a new path for herself. She tells this story through helpful tips and challenges in *The Little Blue Book: A Girl's Guide to Owning Your Professional Development*[18]. Neysha says that her purpose and the full understanding of what allows her to thrive are her dual imperatives, explaining further: "Focusing on the 'what' (my purpose) and the 'how' (what makes me thrive) serves as my compass for most of my decision making. Don't get me wrong, I am not perfect and lose my focus, patience, and poise often. Sometimes I lose my focus several times a day, but by now I can come back to focus relatively quickly with the help of my very tight support system and my meditation practice." For Neysha, the key to making this all work is also her biggest challenge:

> "The biggest challenge is maintaining the discipline of prioritizing self-care during the day. At this point in time my household is relatively respectful of the time when I am behind closed doors in my home office (although I do have to remind them sometimes) and I wake up incredibly early for meditation and exercise. The challenge for me is maintaining the moments of self-care during the day. I call it micro sessions where I shut down and read (or listen to) something uplifting for 5 to 15 min. Sometimes that is incredibly difficult due to the day's demands and I suffer the consequences at home by becoming less patient with the unexpected curveballs that parenthood brings."

Similar to Shannon, and for many of us, making the decision to step out of the more comfortable and predictable career path wasn't as easy as one would like. The scariest part for Neysha, and for many of us, is in the financial implications. Practical as ever, careful planning and living simply allowed for Neysha to fight the fear and make her dream a reality. "I have a sign that says 'Fear kills more dreams than failure ever will'. My twist is that fear is just one of the many options available when you think about your dreams. The women that I am surrounded by (me included) have decided to give it all for their dreams. But that is not the only option either. Just take one small step at a time."

One Small Step for One Woman, One Huge Leap for Others

With all these options out there for women today, there's one option that isn't as celebrated as the others. It's complicated, it's monotonous, and it's messy. There's not a whole lot of glamour or celebration for women who choose to step completely off of the career track and fully embrace homemaking and motherhood, but my God do we need to celebrate it.

Confession: I tried and was not so great at it.

But Mary wow. Mary Wilkerson, a friend I've known since our college days, is doing it. The empire she is building consists of a gaggle of little hands and feet, lost socks, and matching pajamas. I keep up with her pretty regularly, thanks to the wonders of social media, and see the very real, very raw image of her brave woman project that she shares with the world. For she who leads at home, love is in the details.

As Mary herself shares:

"A few years back, I remember switching the laundry and thinking to myself, I will do this thousands and thousands more time before the kids leave home. It almost gave me a panic attack! Doing the same thing every day, just to repeat it the next day, can be a very difficult thing. In addition, very few people understand the work of full-time homemaking and mothering in the modern world, unless they too are full-time homemakers or mothers. This can be difficult because it's the most challenging work I have ever done, but very few people understand that. Leaving my formal career path to become a stay at home mom was an incredibly difficult and unexpected decision. I was well respected and had opportunities in leadership at some of the highest levels in our area when I decided to step away. It was a decision made with a lot of thought, prayer, and discussion with those closest to me. In the end, the type of work I was doing was pulling me away from my family in a way I did not like. In my son's first six months of life, I was out of town for 33 days. I remember thinking, so clearly, my husband and I decided to have children because I wanted to be with them. I wanted to help form them. I wanted to experience every moment I could with them. The pace of life was not something I wanted. 'Busy' is celebrated in today's culture, almost as a god. Success professionally is drilled into our heads from the time we are very young. I knew in the deepest parts of who I am, God wanted me home with my children. Once He speaks to you like that, so clearly, it is impossible to ignore. There were many challenges to me coming home, not the least of which was financial…but my husband and I carved out a plan and worked for two years to provide a path for me to be home with the children. We make sacrifices every day to make it work, but I have never once regretted the time spent with my children, the pace of life which we were able to create for ourselves, and the dreams that we get to live because of the choice to leave full-time ministry. My focus is ensuring I am the person God wants me to be and taking proper care of the people who have been entrusted to me (my children and husband). Becoming this person is a daily choice, and one that is, through my vocation, grounded in service. I have to remind myself, almost daily, that every act of service (cleaning, planning, cooking, packing, changing, etc.) is an opportunity to bring me closer to the person I am suppose to be. For me, staying on focus includes a regimen of daily prayer, carving out time for silence/reflection, and examining my times of failure and my times of success. It's very easy to see the needs of my family as burdens, but when I choose to look at those needs as opportunities to serve the people I love, it becomes more manageable."

In a lot of ways, I think that many women are drawn in to serving others. For she who leads, serving is part of who we are. It's probably because giving of ourselves is baked into our biology as women—every part of our body was designed to nourish and give life to another. Her story, and journey to stay home, wasn't as easy as some might think. I tried it myself, and I wanted to be able to give my children the gift of that time, but it wasn't for us. The financial pressures, the solitude, the emotional stress, and the fear that I wasn't doing it right and that I wasn't being taken seriously by others was just too much for me to bear. I wasn't giving my family my best self, that's for sure. Perhaps, similar to me, finances prohibit you from eliminating an entire income from your household budget. All the stress, worrying about finances and trying to get a baby to sleep, certainly took a toll on my health, both physically and mentally. Back to work I went, but with something different in mind.

Blending a stay at home lifestyle with boss-babing made sense for me, and I had to work to get the harmony of the thing. Let me tell you, Mary's choice is admirable, and her experience of homemaking and giving of herself to her children inspires me, in my time away from work, to live with more reckless abandon in the world of play and grow and love with my own kids and family. In some ways, I think leaving my 15-year career and entering into a couple of years of "create your own adventure" in business was almost as difficult to endure as going through childbirth! It was like jumping from the frying pan into the fire and I was only beginning to understand that.

When I met Kelly Fetick, the co-founder of Landis Consulting Group, a woman-owned business focused on connecting the right people to unique IT challenges, I was already struggling "in the fire". I went from a career that I was okay with, in an environment/culture that I wasn't okay with, to an environment that is viable, and applying boundaries to keep it real! I'm passionate about developing people and helping them live full, effective lives. I do this through coaching and recruiting. But I was really limited in what I was able to do based on where I was. Remember, even though gender equality was something a lot of companies liked to talk about, it wasn't something I was experiencing where I was. Kelly, another working mother of small children, provided me with a calm place to land some of these thoughts.

I wasn't able to spend my talents in ways that really made sense, and I was spinning my wheels trying to make sense of where I was. Other things were suffering, too. I wasn't working out, which was important to me. I wasn't spending enough quality time with my husband, which was important to our family. I wasn't spending enough playtime with our kids, which was important to them. I couldn't get off the hamster wheel of work and guilt, but Kelly's positivity gave me an insight to something else. Kelly's story, in her own words:

"I didn't set out to be a CEO. Quite honestly, I was 10 years into my career and things were going really well. I worked for a smart, leading IT staffing firm, where I'd made a name for myself and truly loved what I did. But I'd reached a crossroads. It was 2014, and my husband and I had just had our first baby and moved across state to my hometown. My company was gracious enough to create a role for me in Pittsburgh and all was seemingly well, but for the first time I found myself questioning the next step in my career. I was a mom now. My priorities had changed. I knew that I loved working, but I was feeling increasingly constricted and needed more autonomy. After a lot of soul searching and counsel from others, the decision to go out on my own was made. Throughout the process I persuaded my sister to join me. She and her husband left NY to move here and the rest is history. Being on this journey with my sister is something I never would've expected and one of the best gifts I've received. Of course we argue, but we share the same values and we're on the same mission. The experience has grown us closer than I ever could've hoped."

Looking back, leaving the comfort and stability of a corporate job was terrifying, and for us the risk and financial implications were huge. It's hard to imagine making the leap without my husband's support. His unwavering belief in me gave me courage then and keeps me going now. Starting and running a company is not for the faint of heart. I focus on the same thing that got me started: my family. Being an entrepreneur requires you to be an optimist. It's so important to remain positive and stay resilient, because you never know what's coming at you the next day. But I wouldn't trade it for the world. I love the freedom and uncapped potential it brings and that I can be my most authentic self every day.

Sustaining an authentically positive outlook in business and life is not easy. Through this tribe of women, I began to realize that restoration and rejuvenation is more about managing energy than about taking vacations. I started small. I bought myself a treadmill and committed to using it regularly. I took more walks outside with a friend. I turned off my phone from 5–8 p.m. nightly and played with my kids. I hired a babysitter to have date nights with my husband. I created a schedule for finishing this book. I took what I knew about myself and developed a priority list based on what I needed to do for what was most important. If I don't know myself, then I can't have the right boundaries for myself and maintain energy. I spent the next eight or nine months in a highly entrepreneurial role and came to realize that it was hard for me to turn off. It was hard to step away and make time for what was most important. I learned that entrepreneurship wasn't totally for me. I place such a high value on task completion and achievement, it doesn't always make sense to be the person who does everything. Burning the candle at both ends will eventually burn it out. Think about where you're at. What energizes you, what depletes you? We all know someone who has suffered a burnout from being in a career that is impossibly unviable. A combination of toxic environment and not being purpose-driven is really tough too.

Perhaps you've heard of Deanna Mulligan, the CEO of Guardian Life Insurance, recently named by *Fortune* magazine as one of the "50 Most Powerful Women in Business"[19] and a repeat member of *Crain's New York Business* list of "The 50 Most Powerful Women in New York".[20] She stepped out of her career for a couple of years and has not only increased the number of people served by Guardian by 400%, but has also made her mark on the bottom line.[21] We can clearly see her successes, but I think her motivation to step out of her career speaks volumes. She began thinking about her impact and legacy, and what difference she was making to the people who mattered most in her life. Including herself. She engaged in periods of solitude and reset. The reset and recharge brought her back stronger than ever. The truth to that is in the numbers I shared. For she who leads, taking care of ourselves and the people who rely on us helps us build strength and energy to do difficult things well.

Discussion/Reflection Questions

Understanding the impact of stress on your body can help you to catch on to key indicators that you are overloaded. Identify five sicknesses, hospitalizations, or times in your life when you were feeling miserable.

Now, identify five key moments that left you feeling overwhelmed and stressed to the max.

What are some of the similarities or differences you can observe from these two areas?

Can you identify a time in your life when you were feeling your best, healthiest, most alive?

"Some women get erased a little at a time, some all
at once. Some reappear. Every woman who appears wrestles
with the forces that would have her disappear. She struggles
with the forces that would tell her story for her, or write
her out of the story, the genealogy, the rights of man, the
rule of law. The ability to tell your own story, in words or
images, is already a victory, already a revolt."

— Rebecca Solnit, *Men Explain Things to Me*[22]

CHAPTER 8

Checking Up and Checking Out

"A 27-year-old is not supposed to have cancer. Cancer, that nasty dream stealer. Cancer, that hope snuffer. Cancer, that old bully. But I did. And I survived. And I didn't lose hope. And I didn't back down. And I'm still fighting. It's the scars though, that really get me.

I'm pretty great at keeping it together, if I do say so myself. I can balance a budget, a household, a workload, a social life. I don't settle for "good enough". I break my back for excellence. The expectation for perfection isn't limited to surface level, but everything I go after. Details, details, details. You name it, I manage it pretty well. And yet here I am, with cancer. That jerk.

But I'm a fighter. A real tough chick. I work like a horse, fight like a pitbull, dress like a lady. I can handle a little pain here and there. Heck, every day for 12 years I handled a little pain. Nearly as frequently, I even handled quite a bit of pain. I didn't slow down. I kept working like a horse, fighting like a pitbull, and dressing like a lady. I just "dealt with it". I saw the docs, took the meds, followed the instructions, endured the colonoscopies, endoscopies, scans, injections, extractions, biopsies, you name it. I was on board. I didn't slow down.

I figured, "This is as good as it gets." I figured, "I have to work a little harder." I figured, "I'm not doing enough, like this, so what else do I have to do?" I wore the makeup, I did my hair, I dressed the part, I hit the gym, I prayed, I worked, and I tried very hard to convince myself (and everyone else) that I was okay.

It wasn't easy. But, then again, I don't do easy. I don't do "good enough." I don't stop.

Then the call came in. Something irregular had shown up. Irregular, even for my particular irregularities. Another round of tests. I didn't slow down. I met the oncology surgeon at his office on a cold winter afternoon; he had kind blue eyes. I don't really recall what he said to me during that visit. I do know that I was ushered down to another office to schedule surgery. It couldn't be that bad, right? I don't remember that conversation at all either. It was my instruction to the Cancer Blur. I just remember looking at my work calendar and trying to figure out if I would be back in time to make those phone calls that were waiting for me."

Reading this entire section from an online journal I kept and later published in a blog still strikes an unpleasant chord. Here I am, ten years, one marriage, and two healthy children later. Stinging. Feeling the lump swell in my throat and the entire computer screen blurring. The scary feeling still challenging me to swallow hard and look up. I'm not sick. I'm not weak. I'm healthy, strong, and living with purpose. But always working, monitoring, thinking about the "what if". But, I can't stop the story there. We can't stop with the uncomfortable truth. Because this is where we learn, this is where we heal:

"Twenty minutes later, I was headed northbound on Route 8 to visit my parents' farm. I was about to tell them that their youngest child had cancer. I was about to shatter their world. A 27-year-old should never have to have that conversation. But I did.

I had that conversation with my best friend, my boyfriend, my boss. I had that conversation so many times that I can't even remember the expressions on their faces. The Cancer Blur.

I busied myself leading up to the day of surgery. The doctor with the kind blue eyes was there. Surgery went well, but then there were the complications. The coding. The vomiting. The tears. The pain. The abscess. The drugs. The haze. I was different. Pieces of me that were once there were taken away. Parts of me that had once been whole were different. The cancer that was growing in me was gone. But what was I left with?

Scars. A whole lot of scars."

The funny thing about scars is this—wait, there's nothing funny about scars. Scars form when there's trauma to a surface. Normally, organs and internal tissues have smooth and slippery surfaces, which allow them to easily move around as the body moves. When there is a trauma affecting these tissues, adhesions (bands of tissue) form and cause tissues and organs to stick together. The actual scar tissue consists of a brittle and substantially more rigid fibrous material. And it ain't pretty to look at.

For the past ten years, I've been preoccupied with the surface scars across my abdomen (and in a number of other puncture and extraction sites along my trunk). I look at the scars every day when I get dressed. The scars that I had to share with my husband when we were married. The scars that grew and changed as I was pregnant with each of my sons. The scars that I have to explain to each new doctor I see. I see visible reminders of a broken body. I feel the tightness of the adhesions underneath. For a long time, I was returning to the place where those scars were wounds. Huge, open wounds.

The open wounds that I was walking around with were, for me, the worst part of it. For most of the time, the Cancer Blur kept me mostly sedated—not quite in touch with the reality and the severity of the place where my plans were changing. But I couldn't hide the open wounds, because thrice daily a nurse or a doctor was poking, prodding, and properly adjusting this part of me that was more tender than I wanted to admit. And the Cancer Blur was broken through in those moments. The body had lessons to teach me. And all these years later, nearly daily, I am reminded of my striving. The striving beauty that I work so hard to attain, maintain, explain. Coming to terms with the scars that my body and soul and mind and memory heal through is essential in my ability to be an authentic woman. For she who leads doesn't leave the scars behind, on another body like a frayed favorite coat stashed in the hall closet. For she who leads, these scars are a very real part of the achievement orientation that pushes, draws, and scares her into the next hard thing. Beneath the surface, the adhesions are binding together, damaging other soft tissue fibers in an effort to build something stronger. But the scars won't ever make it the same as it was. Research proves that scar tissue is actually weaker, less flexible, and actually more prone to future re-injury. And more sensitive to pain than normal, healthy tissue.

The wounds change. Maybe it's a difficult marriage. Maybe it's a sick child or parent. Paralyzing debt. Personal illness. Infertility. A tough job. A period of unemployment. We can't avoid those huge open wounds anymore. We have to talk about them eventually. I have to write about them. For months, my cancer cuts remained opened. For months, multiple sterilizations daily were administered. For months, I was walking around with a gaping hole in the center of my body. I never felt more vulnerable. I never felt more broken. I never felt more hope.

I surprised you there, didn't I?

You see, in the midst of the months of pain and trauma, I still had hope. I was slowly losing the ability to hold it all together. All the time. And I was realizing that maybe I didn't need to hold it all together. All the time. For 12 years I was sick and in pain. Every day. The relief that came from the diagnosis was remarkable.

For months I endured the Cancer Blur, a new kind of pain, with the hope that this suffering too would end. And as I looked at those scars on my stomach, I was proud, knowing that they meant that I had survived. That I was a fighter. That I was a tough chick. And sometimes, even now, when I need to gather some courage, I run my hand over the right side of my body and feel that valley that tells the story of my striving.

But little by little, they got to me. I could feel the pull of the internal scars if I overdid it. I realized that the scars weren't going away. I saw a hollowness in certain outfits. I started to hate my scars. I started to resent the very thing that had once given me hope. And that's when I realized it. My scars reminded me that this perfection that I was always aiming for would never be attainable. In reality, the scars that I wear on my body and in my soul are the very things which make me better than I was, stronger than I thought, braver than I believed, and more whole than ever before. My scars made me someone. Someone perfectly unperfected. For she who leads with scars is already on the other side of the battle. She's already won one.

All this time, I was focused on the "I". Not the how. Not the why. Not the who. I was stuck on the "I"—I have to do this alone. I have to work harder. I have to be more. I have to get better. That was the problem—that was the cancer—that needed to be eradicated from my life. I might be oriented towards achievement and striving and working and wanting and trying.

There was a moment, a very clear moment, when everything changed. I woke up from the Cancer Blur and saw that all this time, I was never ever alone in this. Beyond my family. Beyond my friends. Beyond the multitude of supporters.

All the trying, the focus on perfection, the effort to be "enough," needed to stop. I like to say that God was trying to break my stubborn heart, and I fought him so hard on it that my body broke instead. It was through the broken body that the healing came.

The scars, they are reminders to me of how far I've come. I know now that I was never alone in this. My life has been forever changed, because the focus was shifted. God wants to love me more than He wants to use me. And while it was never about me, it was always about me. About me letting go of the need to hold on to all the control.

My scars? They made me more real. They still do. They made me more whole. Today they remind me that I am not weak. That I can do hard things. We all can. If we dare to try.

Achievement Orientation

Achievement orientation in women is nothing new. As more and more women have entered the workforce and taken on greater responsibilities in society, this achievement orientation has become present. Naturally, the majority of women possess a greater degree of emotional self-awareness and other-awareness. Many women are in a state of hyper-conscientiousness, balancing the present, processing and recalling the past, and anticipating the future. As Jannica Heinström explains in *From Fear to Flow*, "For conscientious persons achievement orientation and goal-directedness color both their thoughts and their emotions around information seeking. Their search experience may appear rational and accompanied by fairly neutral emotions, but they may harbor a strong need to feel competent and successful..."[23] Former bodies of research from the 1970s and 1980s draw women in their state of achievement orientation in a less than ideal light, indicating that there may be greater degrees of dissatisfaction. As a child in the 1980s and 1990s, there was something strange going on. Women were wearing power suits with huge shoulder pads, chanting "If there's anything a man can do, we can do it better" and "I am woman, hear me roar!" I get it; they felt the need and pressure to compete with their male counterparts. But there was something off about it. Rather than compete with male abilities and aptitude, why not complete them? Achievement orientation today paints a different picture, one more balanced in approach, presenting women with this design as open and active in continuous improvement. I'd like to think that the women in this book express and demonstrate openness to continuous improvement. There's a beauty found in the active striving that women who work at getting better bring to the table.

Margaret Mead has noted that the successful or independent woman "is viewed as a hostile and destructive force within society." I like that. I want to bring all my pieces to the rest of the world and change it.

Discussion/Reflection Questions

Can you identify some of the scars in your body or memories that came to mind as you read this chapter? What emotions are you experiencing now?

If you could look back at one of those scars with gratitude, seeing how it made you a bit stronger for the next journey, what would it be and how would you identify it?

What is something you are striving to achieve? How are you approaching it and where is your motivation coming from?

SOMETHING TO PONDER

"Scars have the strange power to remind
us that our past is real."

— Cormac McCarthy, *All the Pretty Horses*[24]

CHAPTER 9

Applying the Stuff

The thing about running is that nobody can do it for you. There's a lot in this book that only you can do. No one can do this work for you. No matter how much someone may want to, they can't.

I really loved running, before I had kids of course. I loved running so much. I'm thinking of the time that I ran my third half marathon. A 13.1 mile experience of serotonin and endorphins, sweat, sunblock, and something called Goo. Gross.

Every year was just a little bit different for me. Year 1: Survive. Finish. And please, God, don't let me have cancer again. Year 2: Finish strong. Run for fun. Be thankful for every mile. With the help of some strong supporters, running with me mile for mile, I completed those two half marathons. It hurt. There were injuries. And, sure enough, there was at least one Lonely Mile in each of those races, when I broke away from the pack, or the pack broke away from me, and I was forced to run. Alone.

There is this mysterious mist that surrounds that word: Alone.

At times, all we want is to be alone. We crave just a half an hour of silence and solitude.

At times, all we want is not to be alone. We crave just a half an hour of adult conversation.

It's funny, though, how rarely we relish those moments in the moment.

That was different for me that time around.

I ran the Lonely Mile. Thirteen times.

Over the year, I've run dozens of 5Ks by myself. I've run many, many training miles by myself. And something has begun to happen. I've started to enjoy those Lonely Miles. I've started to tune in to that little voice inside myself that all along has been saying, "You can do this", "You are strong", "You are a champion".

Over time, that little voice has gotten louder. I've started to believe that I'm a champion. That I'm a finisher. That I'm enough.

So that year, as I endeavored to run that third half marathon, I thought about what made it different. I ran it alone. *Alone.* No friends to run with. No buddies in the trenches. It was me. Nobody could do this for me. And so, for 2 hours and 35 minutes, I ran alone. I discovered that I was/am strong. That I'm a champion. That I'm enough.

You know, that Lonely Mile isn't so scary anymore. It's not so horrible. It's still mysterious though.

Somehow, that Lonely Mile (or 13 Lonely Miles) had the power to put me back together, clear my head, energize me, strengthen me, challenge me, and remind me of how small I am and how large life is. Oddly, that particular race was something I drew on when I was pregnant and in labor with both of my sons. Giving birth (without drugs) (for the first one at least) was one of those power moments that felt like that day so many years ago. Leaving my job and starting something new felt like that too. Losing weight, absolutely. All of it came from that same place inside.

Ladies, let's join together on those Lonely Miles. In our own shoes. On our own roads, trails, and treadmills. Let's dig into that silence, just deep enough to make space to hear that little voice. The one that whispers, "You can do this", "You are strong", "You are a champion". We all know how many other voices are out there telling us other stuff. Forget those voices. The gentle one deep within is the one that fights for you in the Lonely Mile.

Only I can bring my gifts. Only you can bring your gifts. We have to do it, each of us, because we can't do it for each other. For she who leads where she is, is a force, a gale, a tsunami. For she who leads has a story to be told. I want to hear yours. We all do.

Discussion/Reflection Questions

What's the one thing you need to do to tell your story?

What's the one thing that only you can do, that you need to do?

How are you going to do it?

SOMETHING TO PONDER

"You don't need to be helped any longer; you always had the power to go back to Kansas."

— Glinda the Good Witch in *The Wizard of Oz*[25]

Practical Wisdom for She Who Leads

For she who leads is a look inside the souls of women in motion—me, and you.

For she who leads, the first battle is in answering the question, "Am I enough?" and beyond the initial question, it becomes, "What is enough?"

For she who leads, everything matters.

For she who leads, courage and strength is in her DNA.

For she who leads is not alone—she is where she needs to be, with a village of women behind her, an army of warriors beside her, and so many women who have walked before her.

For she who leads, everyone gets served.

For she who leads, running from conflict isn't an option. Nor is stomping our feet and screaming. For she who leads, firming our steps and steadying our chins is necessary for communicating in all ways that we have something important to contribute and we will be making that known.

For she who leads, the environmental red flags are not to be taken lightly.

For she who leads, behaviors have to be rooted in something more than the moment.

For she who leads, courage comes with activating the vision and applying it to decision making.

For she who leads with love, failure, fear, and frustration will threaten to puncture holes in the delicate bags we carry for ourselves and everyone else.

For she who leads, recognizing the difference between dormant and done is important for our own growth.

For she who leads, being honest about endings builds endurance.

For she who leads, resisting fear as a motivator makes us stronger.

For she who leads with heart, there's really no fear of failure.

For she who leads like me, bless your heart. Burnout is right around the corner, waiting for you to trip in those fabulously appointed heels and wide-leg dress pants.

For she who leads, learning how to harness your strengths and apply them to the work before you will do you well in life, and in business, opening the door for the things you desire most.

For she who leads at home, love is in the details.

For she who leads, serving is part of who we are.

For she who leads, taking care of ourselves and the people who rely on us helps us build strength and energy to do difficult things well.

For she who leads with scars is already on the other side of the battle.

For she who leads where she is, is a force, a gale, a tsunami.

For she who leads has a story to be told.

References

1. Clance, P. R., & Imea, S. (1978). The Impostor Phenomenon in High Achieving Women: Dynamics and Therapeutic Intervention. *Psychotherapy: Theory, Research and Practice*,15(3). Retrieved from http://www.paulineroseclance.com/pdf/ip_high_achieving_women.pdf

2. Stillman, J. (2018, June29). Impostor Syndrome Affects Men and Women Differently. Retrieved from https://curiosity.com/topics/impostor-syndrome-affects-men-and-women-differently-curiosity/

3. Clance, P. R. (n.d.). Impostor Phenomenon. Retrieved from https://paulineroseclance.com/impostor_phenomenon.html

4. Hooks, B. (2002). *Communion: The Female Search for Love*. New York, NY: William Morrow.

5. Hansan, J. (2011). Lucy Burns (1879-1966): Suffragette and Militant Activist on Behalf of Women's Rights. Retrieved from http://socialwelfare.library.vcu.edu/people/burns-lucy/

6. Catalyst. (2019, December 4). Pyramid: Women in S&P 500 Companies. Retrieved from https://www.catalyst.org/research/women-in-sp-500-companies/

7. Ortiz, J. L. (2018, October 4). Will #MeToo turn into #NotHer? Movement may come with unintended workplace consequences. Retrieved from https://www.usatoday.com/story/news/2018/10/04/metoo-movement-unintended-career-consequences-women/1503516002/

8. HuffPost. (2012, June26). Nora Ephron's Commencement Address To Wellesley Class Of 1996. Retrieved from https://www.huffpost.com/entry/norah-ephrons-commencement-96-address_n_1628832

9. Adichie, C. N. (2015). *We Should All Be Feminists*. New York, NY: Anchor.

10. Cloud, H., & Townsend, J. (2018). *Boundaries: When to Say Yes, How to Say No to Take Control of Your Life.* Grand Rapids, MI: Zondervan.

11. Dowling, C. (1982). *The Cinderella Complex: Women's Hidden Fear of Independence.* Pocket Books.

12. Janssen, S. (2007, November 30). Quote Check: Mark Twain Birthday Edition. Retrieved from http://www.worldalmanac.com/blog/2007/11/quote_check_mark_twain_birthda.html

13. Goldman, B. (2017). Two minds: The cognitive differences between men and women. Stanford Medicine. Retrieved from https://stanmed.stanford.edu/2017spring/how-mens-and-womens-brains-are-different.html

14. Karlgaard, R. (2019). *Late Bloomers: The Power of Patience in a World Obsessed with Early Achievement.* New York, NY: Currency.

15. Siena, S. C. (2007). *Dialogue of St. Catherine of Siena*. New York, NY: Cosimo.

16. Stein, E. (2012). *Essays on Woman (The Collected Works of Edith Stein)*. ICS Publications.

17. Gregg, S. J., & McBride, R. S. (2017). *It's About Time: How to Do More of What Matters with the Time You Have*. Retrieved from https://timemagicment.com/book/

18. Arcelay, N. (2019). *The Little Blue Book: A girl's guide to owning your professional development*. Retrieved from https://www.amazon.com/Little-Blue-Book-professional-development/dp/1070660426

19. Fortune. (2017, September21). 50 Most Powerful Women in Business: Deanna Mulligan. Retrieved from https://fortune.com/most-powerful-women/2017/deanna-mulligan/

20. Deffenbaugh, R. (2019). Most Powerful Women -15. Deanna Mulligan. Retrieved from https://www.crainsnewyork.com/awards/most-powerful-women-2019-deanna-mulligan

21. Cutter, C. (2019, October13). She Took a Two-Year Break in Her Career. Now She's CEO. Retrieved from https://www.msn.com/cn us/news/us/she-took-a-two-year-break-in-her-career-now-shes-ceo/ar-AAICL10

22. Solnit, R. (2014). *Men Explain Things to Me*. Haymarket Books.

23. Heinstrom, J. (2010). *From Fear to Flow: Personality and Information Interaction*. Amsterdam, Netherlands: Elsevier.

24. McCarthy, C. (1993). *All the Pretty Horses*. New York, NY: Vintage.

25. Fleming, V. (Director). (1939). *The Wizard of Oz* [Motion picture]. United States: Metro-Goldwyn-Mayer.

About the Author

Holly Joy McIlwain graduated from Franciscan University in Steubenville in 2003 and spent years working with young people and families, schools, churches, health clubs, salons, and really anywhere that people gathered and talked about what was most important to them.

After an exciting decade and a half of working, traveling, dating, and exploring all the best (and worst) parts of life, she met her husband Kevin, settled down, and got married. Just like that she became a mother, too! In heroic pursuit of a master's degree at the ripe old age of 30-something, and pregnant again, she began rethinking career goals and created something different on her imaginary vision board. A hater of pop-psychology, lover of philosophy, and big time nerd about behavior sciences, Holly finished her master's degree at Robert Morris University, had that beautiful second baby, and moved for the third (or fourth?) time since marrying the one who gave her the sweet last name (pronounced Mac-Ill-wane).

Holly spends her days being a mom to two rambunctious and amazing boys, working in the leadership development and talent industry, and living life to the fullest. Holly's been speaking and writing for nearly 20 years and can't believe this is her first book.

You can follow her with the hashtag **#bravewomenproject** and learn more about her adventures in business, motherhood, and all things ketogenic. Want even more? Email her at **HollyJoyMcilwain@gmail.com** and give her a piece of your own mind.